MznLnx

Missing Links Exam Preps

Exam Prep for

Essentials of Marketing Research

Kumar & Aaker & Day, 2nd Edition

The MznLnx Exam Prep is your link from the texbook and lecture to your exams.
The MznLnx Exam Preps are unauthorized and comprehensive reviews of your textbooks.

All material provided by MznLnx and Rico Publications (c) 2010
Textbook publishers and textbook authors do not particpate in or contribute to these reviews.

MznLnx

Rico
Publications

Exam Prep for Essentials of Marketing Research
2nd Edition
Kumar & Aaker & Day

Publisher: Raymond Houge
Assistant Editor: Michael Rouger
Text and Cover Designer: Lisa Buckner
Marketing Manager: Sara Swagger
Project Manager, Editorial Production: Jerry Emerson
Art Director: Vernon Lowerui

Product Manager: Dave Mason
Editorial Asitant: Rachel Guzmanji
Pedagogy: Debra Long
Cover Image: Jim Reed/Getty Images
Text and Cover Printer: City Printing, Inc.
Compositor: Media Mix, Inc.

(c) 2010 Rico Publications

ALL RIGHTS RESERVED. No part of this work covered by the copyright may be reproduced or used in any form or by an means--graphic, electronic, or mechanical, including photocopying, recording, taping, Web distribution, information storage, and retrieval systems, or in any other manner--without the written permission of the publisher.

Printed in the United States
ISBN:

For more information about our products, contact us at:
Dave.Mason@RicoPublications.com

For permission to use material from this text or product, submit a request online to:
Dave.Mason@RicoPublications.com

Contents

CHAPTER 1
A Decision-Marking Perspective on Marketing Research — 1

CHAPTER 2
Marketing Research in Practice — 7

CHAPTER 3
The Marketing Research Process — 13

CHAPTER 4
Research Design and Implementation — 17

CHAPTER 5
Secondary and Standardized Sources of Marketing Data — 27

CHAPTER 6
Marketing Research on the Internet — 38

CHAPTER 7
Information Collection: Qualitative and Observational Methods — 44

CHAPTER 8
Information from Respondents: Issues in Data Collection — 51

CHAPTER 9
Attitude Measurement — 59

CHAPTER 10
Designing the Questionnaire — 64

CHAPTER 11
Sampling Fundamentals — 68

CHAPTER 12
Fundamentals of Data Analysis — 78

CHAPTER 13
Hypothesis Testing — 86

CHAPTER 14
Correlation Analysis and Regression Analysis — 95

CHAPTER 15
Presenting the Results — 102

CHAPTER 16
Applications of Marketing Research — 103

ANSWER KEY — 122

TO THE STUDENT

COMPREHENSIVE

The *MznLnx* Exam Prep series is designed to help you pass your exams. Editors at MznLnx review your textbooks and then prepare these practice exams to help you master the textbook material. Unlike study guides, workbooks, and practice tests provided by the texbook publisher and textbook authors, *MznLnx* gives you **all** of the material in each chapter in exam form, not just samples, so you can be sure to nail your exam.

MECHANICAL

The MznLnx Exam Prep series creates exams that will help you learn the subject matter as well as test you on your understanding. Each question is designed to help you master the concept. Just working through the exams, you gain an understanding of the subject--its a simple mechanical process that produces success.

INTEGRATED STUDY GUIDE AND REVIEW

MznLnx is not just a set of exams designed to test you, its also a comprehensive review of the subject content. Each exam question is also a review of the concept, making sure that you will get the answer correct without having to go to other sources of material. You learn as you go! Its the easiest way to pass an exam.

HUMOR

Studying can be tedious and dry. MznLnx's instructional design includes moderate humor within the exam questions on occassion, to break the tedium and revitalize the brain

Chapter 1. A Decision-Marking Perspective on Marketing Research

1. _____ is defined by the American _____ Association as the activity, set of institutions, and processes for creating, communicating, delivering, and exchanging offerings that have value for customers, clients, partners, and society at large. The term developed from the original meaning which referred literally to going to market, as in shopping, or going to a market to sell goods or services.

_____ practice tends to be seen as a creative industry, which includes advertising, distribution and selling.

   a. Business marketing
   b. Gatefold
   c. Marketing
   d. Product naming

2. Consumer market research is a form of applied sociology that concentrates on understanding the behaviours, whims and preferences, of consumers in a market-based economy, and aims to understand the effects and comparative success of marketing campaigns. The field of consumer _____ as a statistical science was pioneered by Arthur Nielsen with the founding of the ACNielsen Company in 1923 .

Thus _____ is the systematic and objective identification, collection, analysis, and dissemination of information for the purpose of assisting management in decision making related to the identification and solution of problems and opportunities in marketing.

   a. Market analysis
   b. Logit analysis
   c. Simple random sampling
   d. Marketing research

3. _____ is an independent technology and market research company that provides its clients with advice about technology's impact on business and consumers. _____ has four research centers in the US: Cambridge, Massachusetts; Foster City, California; Washington, D.C.; and Westport, Connecticut. It also has four European research centers in Amsterdam, Frankfurt, London, and Paris.
   a. Checkoff
   b. Forrester Research
   c. National Asset Recovery Services
   d. Mapinfo

4. _____/primary market research has traditionally been thought different from methods of research conducted in a laboratory or academic setting. It was developed originally from anthropology and is sometimes know as participant research, or as ethnography in anthropology

Chapter 1. A Decision-Marking Perspective on Marketing Research

a. Mystery shoppers
b. Mystery shopping
c. Market research
d. Field Research

5. _____ is a marketing term, and involves evaluating the situation and trends in a particular company's market. _____ is often called the 'three c's', which refers to the three major elements that must be studied:

- Customers
- Costs
- Competition

The number of 'c's' is sometimes extended to four, five, or even six, with 'Collaboration', 'Company', and 'Competitive advantage'.

- Marketing mix
- SWOT analysis

a. 6-3-5 Brainwriting
b. Power III
c. Situation analysis
d. 180SearchAssistant

6. A _____ is a plan of action designed to achieve a particular goal.

_____ is different from tactics. In military terms, tactics is concerned with the conduct of an engagement while _____ is concerned with how different engagements are linked.

a. Power III
b. Strategy
c. 6-3-5 Brainwriting
d. 180SearchAssistant

7. _____ is a rivalry between individuals, groups, nations for territory, a niche, or allocation of resources. It arises whenever two or more parties strive for a goal which cannot be shared. _____ occurs naturally between living organisms which co-exist in the same environment.

a. Price fixing
b. Non-price competition
c. Direct competition
d. Competition

8. _____ is the realization of an application idea, model, design, specification, standard, algorithm an _____ is a realization of a technical specification or algorithm as a program, software component, or other computer system. Many _____s may exist for a given specification or standard.
a. ADTECH
b. Implementation
c. AMAX
d. ACNielsen

9. _____ is a term that refers both to:

- a formal discipline used to help appraise, or assess, the case for a project or proposal, which itself is a process known as project appraisal; and
- an informal approach to making decisions of any kind.

Under both definitions the process involves, whether explicitly or implicitly, weighing the total expected costs against the total expected benefits of one or more actions in order to choose the best or most profitable option. The formal process is often referred to as either CBA (_____) or BCost-benefit analysis

A hallmark of CBA is that all benefits and all costs are expressed in money terms, and are adjusted for the time value of money, so that all flows of benefits and flows of project costs over time (which tend to occur at different points in time) are expressed on a common basis in terms of their 'present value.' Closely related, but slightly different, formal techniques include Cost-effectiveness analysis, Economic impact analysis, Fiscal impact analysis and Social Return on Investment(SROI) analysis. The latter builds upon the logic of _____, but differs in that it is explicitly designed to inform the practical decision-making of enterprise managers and investors focused on optimising their social and environmental impacts.

a. 6-3-5 Brainwriting
b. 180SearchAssistant
c. Cost-benefit analysis
d. Power III

Chapter 1. A Decision-Marking Perspective on Marketing Research

10. Procter is a surname, and may also refer to:

- Bryan Waller Procter (pseud. Barry Cornwall), English poet
- Goodwin Procter, American law firm
- _____, consumer products multinational

a. Procter ' Gamble
b. Comparison-Shopping agent
c. Push
d. Developed country

11. _____ , according to Cornish, 'the process of acquiring and analyzing information in order to understand the market (both existing and potential customers); to determine the current and future needs and preferences, attitudes and behavior of the market; and to assess changes in the business environment that may affect the size and nature of the market in the future.' ('Product', 1997, p147.)

This figure shows how the interaction between variables from producers, communication channels, and consumers vary the effectiveness of _____ which affects the performance of the sales of a new product. The product is central in a circle because it helps to direct what information is gathered and how.

a. Co-branding
b. Brand parity
c. Specialty catalogs
d. Market intelligence

12. _____ is a branch of philosophy which seeks to address questions about morality, such as how a moral outcome can be achieved in a specific situation (applied _____), how moral values should be determined (normative _____), what moral values people actually abide by (descriptive _____), what the fundamental semantic, ontological, and epistemic nature of _____ or morality is (meta-_____), and how moral capacity or moral agency develops and what its nature is (moral psychology.)

Socrates was one of the first Greek philosophers to encourage both scholars and the common citizen to turn their attention from the outside world to the condition of man. In this view, Knowledge having a bearing on human life was placed highest, all other knowledge being secondary.

a. ADTECH
b. AMAX
c. ACNielsen
d. Ethics

13. Founded in 1957, the _____ is one of the largest trade associations of market research and polling professionals. _____ has more than 3,000 members worldwide, representing all segments of the research industry. _____ advances, protects and promotes knowledge, standards, excellence, ethics, professional development and innovation for the global market and opinion research profession.
   a. PRSA
   b. Power III
   c. 180SearchAssistant
   d. Marketing Research Association

14. A supply chain is the system of organizations, people, technology, activities, information and resources involved in moving a product or service from _____ to customer. Supply chain activities transform natural resources, raw materials and components into a finished product that is delivered to the end customer. In sophisticated supply chain systems, used products may re-enter the supply chain at any point where residual value is recyclable.
   a. Relationship Management Application
   b. Little value placed on potential benefits
   c. GE matrix
   d. Supplier

15. _____ a research method involving the use of questionnaires and/or statistical surveys to gather data about people and their thoughts and behaviours.
   a. Stratified sampling
   b. Randomization
   c. Control chart
   d. Survey Research

16. _____ is the principle that an institution or individual should not reveal information about their clients to a third party without the consent of the client or a clear legal reason. This concept is commonly provided for in law in most countries.

The access to a client's data as provided by the institution in question is usually limited to law enforcement agencies and requires some legal procedures to be accomplished prior to such action (eg.: court order issued, etc.).

   a. 180SearchAssistant
   b. 6-3-5 Brainwriting
   c. Power III
   d. Client confidentiality

17. _____ is the ability of an individual or group to seclude themselves or information about themselves and thereby reveal themselves selectively. The boundaries and content of what is considered private differ among cultures and individuals, but share basic common themes. _____ is sometimes related to anonymity, the wish to remain unnoticed or unidentified in the public realm.
   a. 6-3-5 Brainwriting
   b. Power III
   c. 180SearchAssistant
   d. Privacy

18. _____ has been defined by the International Organization for Standardization (ISO) as 'ensuring that information is accessible only to those authorized to have access' and is one of the cornerstones of information security. _____ is one of the design goals for many cryptosystems, made possible in practice by the techniques of modern cryptography.

   _____ also refers to an ethical principle associated with several professions (e.g., medicine, law, religion, professional psychology, and journalism.)

   a. 6-3-5 Brainwriting
   b. Confidentiality
   c. 180SearchAssistant
   d. Power III

19. According to the American Marketing Association, _____ is the marketing of products that are presumed to be environmentally safe. Thus _____ incorporates a broad range of activities, including product modification, changes to the production process, packaging changes, as well as modifying advertising. Yet defining _____ is not a simple task where several meanings intersect and contradict each other; an example of this will be the existence of varying social, environmental and retail definitions attached to this term.
   a. Market segment
   b. Perceptual mapping
   c. Green marketing
   d. Customer analytics

Chapter 2. Marketing Research in Practice

1. _____ is a genre of writing that uses fieldwork to provide a descriptive study of human societies. _____ presents the results of a holistic research method founded on the idea that a system's properties cannot necessarily be accurately understood independently of each other. The genre has both formal and historical connections to travel writing and colonial office reports.
    a. ADTECH
    b. ACNielsen
    c. Ethnography
    d. AMAX

2. _____ is defined by the American _____ Association as the activity, set of institutions, and processes for creating, communicating, delivering, and exchanging offerings that have value for customers, clients, partners, and society at large. The term developed from the original meaning which referred literally to going to market, as in shopping, or going to a market to sell goods or services.

    _____ practice tends to be seen as a creative industry, which includes advertising, distribution and selling.

    a. Product naming
    b. Business marketing
    c. Marketing
    d. Gatefold

3. _____ , according to Cornish, 'the process of acquiring and analyzing information in order to understand the market (both existing and potential customers); to determine the current and future needs and preferences, attitudes and behavior of the market; and to assess changes in the business environment that may affect the size and nature of the market in the future.' ('Product', 1997, p147.)

    This figure shows how the interaction between variables from producers, communication channels, and consumers vary the effectiveness of _____ which affects the performance of the sales of a new product. The product is central in a circle because it helps to direct what information is gathered and how.

    a. Co-branding
    b. Brand parity
    c. Specialty catalogs
    d. Market intelligence

4. A _____ is a structured collection of records or data that is stored in a computer system. The structure is achieved by organizing the data according to a _____ model. The model in most common use today is the relational model.

a. Power III
b. Database
c. 6-3-5 Brainwriting
d. 180SearchAssistant

5. Consumer market research is a form of applied sociology that concentrates on understanding the behaviours, whims and preferences, of consumers in a market-based economy, and aims to understand the effects and comparative success of marketing campaigns. The field of consumer _____ as a statistical science was pioneered by Arthur Nielsen with the founding of the ACNielsen Company in 1923 .

Thus _____ is the systematic and objective identification, collection, analysis, and dissemination of information for the purpose of assisting management in decision making related to the identification and solution of problems and opportunities in marketing.

a. Marketing research
b. Logit analysis
c. Market analysis
d. Simple random sampling

6. _____ is a form of direct marketing using databases of customers or potential customers to generate personalized communications in order to promote a product or service for marketing purposes. The method of communication can be any addressable medium, as in direct marketing.

The distinction between direct and _____ stems primarily from the attention paid to the analysis of data.

a. Direct Marketing Associations
b. Direct marketing
c. Power III
d. Database Marketing

7. A supply chain is the system of organizations, people, technology, activities, information and resources involved in moving a product or service from _____ to customer. Supply chain activities transform natural resources, raw materials and components into a finished product that is delivered to the end customer. In sophisticated supply chain systems, used products may re-enter the supply chain at any point where residual value is recyclable.
a. GE matrix
b. Relationship Management Application
c. Supplier
d. Little value placed on potential benefits

Chapter 2. Marketing Research in Practice

8. _____ refers to the production of some commodity or service, such as a television program, using a company's own funds, staff, or resources.

This is in contrast to production being outsourced (contracted out) to another company.

- Proprietary

a. Outsourcing
b. Intangible assets
c. ACNielsen
d. In-house

9. In economics, an externality or spillover of an economic transaction is an impact on a party that is not directly involved in the transaction. In such a case, prices do not reflect the full costs or benefits in production or consumption of a product or service. A positive impact is called an _____ benefit, while a negative impact is called an _____ cost.

a. ADTECH
b. ACNielsen
c. AMAX
d. External

10. An _____ is the manufacturing of a good or service within a category. Although _____ is a broad term for any kind of economic production, in economics and urban planning _____ is a synonym for the secondary sector, which is a type of economic activity involved in the manufacturing of raw materials into goods and products.

There are four key industrial economic sectors: the primary sector, largely raw material extraction industries such as mining and farming; the secondary sector, involving refining, construction, and manufacturing; the tertiary sector, which deals with services (such as law and medicine) and distribution of manufactured goods; and the quaternary sector, a relatively new type of knowledge _____ focusing on technological research, design and development such as computer programming, and biochemistry.

a. AMAX
b. ADTECH
c. Industry
d. ACNielsen

11. _____ a research method involving the use of questionnaires and/or statistical surveys to gather data about people and their thoughts and behaviours.

a. Control chart
b. Survey Research
c. Stratified sampling
d. Randomization

12. _____ often refers to either primary or secondary research. Secondary research involves a company using information compiled from various sources, which is about a new or existing product. The advantages of secondary research are that it is relatively cheap and easily accessible.
   a. Questionnaire
   b. Mystery shopping
   c. Mystery shoppers
   d. Market Research

13. _____ is an advertisement in which a particular product specifically mentions a competitor by name for the express purpose of showing why the competitor is inferior to the product naming it.

This should not be confused with parody advertisements, where a fictional product is being advertised for the purpose of poking fun at the particular advertisement, nor should it be confused with the use of a coined brand name for the purpose of comparing the product without actually naming an actual competitor. ('Wikipedia tastes better and is less filling than the Encyclopedia Galactica.')

In the 1980s, during what has been referred to as the cola wars, soft-drink manufacturer Pepsi ran a series of advertisements where people, caught on hidden camera, in a blind taste test, chose Pepsi over rival Coca-Cola.

   a. GL-70
   b. Cost per conversion
   c. Heavy-up
   d. Comparative advertising

14. A number of different _____s are indicated below.

- Randomized controlled trial
    - Double-blind randomized trial
    - Single-blind randomized trial
    - Non-blind trial
- Nonrandomized trial (quasi-experiment)
    - Interrupted time series design (measures on a sample or a series of samples from the same population are obtained several times before and after a manipulated event or a naturally occurring event) - considered a type of quasi-experiment

- Cohort study
    - Prospective cohort
    - Retrospective cohort
    - Time series study
- Case-control study
    - Nested case-control study
- Cross-sectional study
    - Community survey (a type of cross-sectional study)

When choosing a _____, many factors must be taken into account. Different types of studies are subject to different types of bias. For example, recall bias is likely to occur in cross-sectional or case-control studies where subjects are asked to recall exposure to risk factors.

a. Power III
b. Longitudinal studies
c. Study design
d. 180SearchAssistant

15. _____ is a measure of the strength of a brand, product, service relative to competitive offerings. There is often a geographic element to the competitive landscape. In defining _____, you must see to what extent a product, brand, or firm controls a product category in a given geographic area.

a. Discretionary spending
b. Productivity
c. Market system
d. Market dominance

16. Human beings are also considered to be _____ because they have the ability to change raw materials into valuable _____. The term Human _____ can also be defined as the skills, energies, talents, abilities and knowledge that are used for the production of goods or the rendering of services. While taking into account human beings as _____, the following things have to be kept in mind:

- The size of the population
- The capabilities of the individuals in that population

Many _____ cannot be consumed in their original form. They have to be processed in order to change them into more usable commodities.

a. 6-3-5 Brainwriting
b. 180SearchAssistant
c. Power III
d. Resources

Chapter 3. The Marketing Research Process

1. _____ is defined by the American _____ Association as the activity, set of institutions, and processes for creating, communicating, delivering, and exchanging offerings that have value for customers, clients, partners, and society at large. The term developed from the original meaning which referred literally to going to market, as in shopping, or going to a market to sell goods or services.

_____ practice tends to be seen as a creative industry, which includes advertising, distribution and selling.

a. Product naming
b. Business marketing
c. Gatefold
d. Marketing

2. Consumer market research is a form of applied sociology that concentrates on understanding the behaviours, whims and preferences, of consumers in a market-based economy, and aims to understand the effects and comparative success of marketing campaigns. The field of consumer _____ as a statistical science was pioneered by Arthur Nielsen with the founding of the ACNielsen Company in 1923 .

Thus _____ is the systematic and objective identification, collection, analysis, and dissemination of information for the purpose of assisting management in decision making related to the identification and solution of problems and opportunities in marketing.

a. Simple random sampling
b. Logit analysis
c. Marketing research
d. Market analysis

3. _____ is a set of six steps which defines the tasks to be accomplished in conducting a marketing research study. These include problem definition, developing an approach to problem, research design formulation, field work, data preparation and analysis, and report generation and presentation.
a. Simple random sampling
b. Focus group
c. Marketing research process
d. Market analysis

4. A number of different _____s are indicated below.

- Randomized controlled trial
    - Double-blind randomized trial
    - Single-blind randomized trial
    - Non-blind trial
- Nonrandomized trial (quasi-experiment)
    - Interrupted time series design (measures on a sample or a series of samples from the same population are obtained several times before and after a manipulated event or a naturally occurring event) - considered a type of quasi-experiment
- Cohort study
    - Prospective cohort
    - Retrospective cohort
    - Time series study
- Case-control study
    - Nested case-control study
- Cross-sectional study
    - Community survey (a type of cross-sectional study)

When choosing a _____, many factors must be taken into account. Different types of studies are subject to different types of bias. For example, recall bias is likely to occur in cross-sectional or case-control studies where subjects are asked to recall exposure to risk factors.

a. 180SearchAssistant
b. Longitudinal studies
c. Power III
d. Study design

5. A personal and cultural _____ is a relative ethic _____, an assumption upon which implementation can be extrapolated. A _____ system is a set of consistent _____s and measures that is soo not true. A principle _____ is a foundation upon which other _____s and measures of integrity are based.
a. Dolly Dimples
b. Customization
c. Private branding
d. Value

6. Advertising mail junk mail is the delivery of advertising material to recipients of postal mail. The delivery of advertising mail forms a large and growing service for many postal services, and _____ marketing forms a significant portion of the direct marketing industry. Some organizations attempt to help people opt-out of receiving advertising mail, in many cases motivated by a concern over its negative environmental impact.

Chapter 3. The Marketing Research Process

a. Phishing
b. Telemarketing
c. Direct mail
d. Directory Harvest Attack

7. In probability theory and statistics, the _____ (or expectation value or mean and for continuous random variables with a density function it is the probability density -weighted integral of the possible values.

The term '_____' can be misleading.

a. ACNielsen
b. AMAX
c. ADTECH
d. Expected value

8. In decision theory, the _____ is the price that one would be willing to pay in order to gain access to perfect information.

The problem is modeled with a payoff matrix R_{ij} in which the row index i describes a choice that must be made by the payer, while the column index j describes a random variable that the payer does not yet have knowledge of, that has probability p_j of being in state j. If the payer is to choose i without knowing the value of j, the best choice is the one that maximizes the expected monetary value:

$$\boxed{}$$

where

$$\boxed{}$$

is the expected payoff for action i i.e. the expectation value, and

$$\boxed{}$$

is choosing the maximum of these expectations for all available actions.

a. ADTECH
b. AMAX
c. Expected value of perfect information
d. ACNielsen

Chapter 4. Research Design and Implementation

1. _____ refer to a collection of facts usually collected as the result of experience, observation or experiment or a set of premises. This may consist of numbers, words particularly as measurements or observations of a set of variables. _____ are often viewed as a lowest level of abstraction from which information and knowledge are derived.
   a. P-Value
   b. Median
   c. Randomization
   d. Data

2. _____ is a term used to describe a process of preparing and collecting data - for example as part of a process improvement or similar project.

   _____ usually takes place early on in an improvement project, and is often formalised through a _____ Plan which often contains the following activity.

   1. Pre collection activity - Agree goals, target data, definitions, methods
   2. Collection - _____
   3. Present Findings - usually involves some form of sorting analysis and/or presentation.

   A formal _____ process is necessary as it ensures that data gathered is both defined and accurate and that subsequent decisions based on arguments embodied in the findings are valid. The process provides both a baseline from which to measure from and in certain cases a target on what to improve. Types of _____ 1-By mail questionnaires 2-By personal interview

   - Six sigma
   - Sampling (statistics)

   a. Data collection
   b. Power III
   c. 6-3-5 Brainwriting
   d. 180SearchAssistant

Chapter 4. Research Design and Implementation

3. A number of different _____s are indicated below.

- Randomized controlled trial
  - Double-blind randomized trial
  - Single-blind randomized trial
  - Non-blind trial
- Nonrandomized trial (quasi-experiment)
  - Interrupted time series design (measures on a sample or a series of samples from the same population are obtained several times before and after a manipulated event or a naturally occurring event) - considered a type of quasi-experiment

- Cohort study
  - Prospective cohort
  - Retrospective cohort
  - Time series study
- Case-control study
  - Nested case-control study
- Cross-sectional study
  - Community survey (a type of cross-sectional study)

When choosing a _____, many factors must be taken into account. Different types of studies are subject to different types of bias. For example, recall bias is likely to occur in cross-sectional or case-control studies where subjects are asked to recall exposure to risk factors.

a. Power III
b. 180SearchAssistant
c. Longitudinal studies
d. Study design

4. _____ is a type of research conducted because a problem has not been clearly defined. _____ helps determine the best research design, data collection method and selection of subjects. Given its fundamental nature, _____ often concludes that a perceived problem does not actually exist.
a. ACNielsen
b. IDDEA
c. Intent scale translation
d. Exploratory research

5. _____ describes data and characteristics about the population or phenomenon being studied. _____ answers the questions who, what, where, when and how.

Although the data description is factual, accurate and systematic, the research cannot describe what caused a situation.

Chapter 4. Research Design and Implementation 19

a. Power III
b. Varimax rotation
c. Sampling error
d. Descriptive research

6. _____ is one of the four Ps of the marketing mix. The other three aspects are product, promotion, and place. It is also a key variable in microeconomic price allocation theory.

a. Transfer pricing
b. Pricing
c. Cost-plus pricing
d. Resale price maintenance

7. Procter is a surname, and may also refer to:

- Bryan Waller Procter (pseud. Barry Cornwall), English poet
- Goodwin Procter, American law firm
- _____, consumer products multinational

a. Push
b. Comparison-Shopping agent
c. Developed country
d. Procter ' Gamble

8. A _____ is a plan of action designed to achieve a particular goal.

_____ is different from tactics. In military terms, tactics is concerned with the conduct of an engagement while _____ is concerned with how different engagements are linked.

a. 180SearchAssistant
b. Strategy
c. 6-3-5 Brainwriting
d. Power III

9. _____ is a term for unprocessed data, it is also known as primary data. It is a relative term _____ can be input to a computer program or used in manual analysis procedures such as gathering statistics from a survey.

Chapter 4. Research Design and Implementation

a. Shoppers Food ' Pharmacy
b. Product manager
c. Raw data
d. Chief marketing officer

10. Combining Existing _____ Sources with New Primary Data Sources

Imagine that we could get hold of a good collection of surveys taken in earlier years, such as detailed studies about changes going on in this phase and hopefully additional studies in the years to come. Analyzing this data base over time could give us a good picture of what changes actually have taken place in the orientation of the population and of the extent to which new technical concepts did have an impact on subgroups of the population. Furthermore, data archives can help to prepare studies on change over time by monitoring what questions have been asked in earlier years and alerting principal investigators to important questions which should be repeated in planned research projects.

a. Power III
b. 6-3-5 Brainwriting
c. 180SearchAssistant
d. Secondary data

11. _____ is that part of statistical practice concerned with the selection of individual observations intended to yield some knowledge about a population of concern, especially for the purposes of statistical inference. Each observation measures one or more properties (weight, location, etc.) of an observable entity enumerated to distinguish objects or individuals.

a. Richard Buckminster 'Bucky' Fuller
b. AStore
c. Sports Marketing Group
d. Sampling

12. _____ is the realization of an application idea, model, design, specification, standard, algorithm an _____ is a realization of a technical specification or algorithm as a program, software component, or other computer system. Many _____ s may exist for a given specification or standard.

a. ADTECH
b. ACNielsen
c. AMAX
d. Implementation

Chapter 4. Research Design and Implementation

13. _____ in economics and business is the result of an exchange and from that trade we assign a numerical monetary value to a good, service or asset. If I trade 4 apples for an orange, the _____ of an orange is 4 - apples. Inversely, the _____ of an apple is 1/4 oranges.
   a. Contribution margin-based pricing
   b. Price war
   c. Price
   d. Transfer pricing

14. A personal and cultural _____ is a relative ethic _____, an assumption upon which implementation can be extrapolated. A _____ system is a set of consistent _____s and measures that is soo not true. A principle _____ is a foundation upon which other _____s and measures of integrity are based.
   a. Customization
   b. Private branding
   c. Dolly Dimples
   d. Value

15. _____ generally refers to a list of all planned expenses and revenues. It is a plan for saving and spending. A _____ is an important concept in microeconomics, which uses a _____ line to illustrate the trade-offs between two or more goods.
   a. Power III
   b. 180SearchAssistant
   c. Budget
   d. 6-3-5 Brainwriting

16. The _____, abbreviated _____ is a mathematically based algorithm for scheduling a set of project activities. It is an important tool for effective project management.

It was developed in the 1950s by the US Navy when trying to better organize the building of submarines and later, especially, when building nuclear submarines.

   a. Critical path method
   b. 180SearchAssistant
   c. 6-3-5 Brainwriting
   d. Power III

17. A _____ is a type of bar chart that illustrates a project schedule. A _____ illustrates the start and finish dates of the terminal elements and summary elements of a project. Terminal elements and summary elements comprise the work breakdown structure of the project.

Chapter 4. Research Design and Implementation

a. 180SearchAssistant
b. 6-3-5 Brainwriting
c. Power III
d. GANTT chart

18. The _____, is a model for project management designed to analyze and represent the tasks involved in completing a given project.

_____ is a method to analyze the involved tasks in completing a given project, especially the time needed to complete each task, and identifying the minimum time needed to complete the total project.

PERT was developed primarily to simplify the planning and scheduling of large and complex projects.

a. 180SearchAssistant
b. 6-3-5 Brainwriting
c. Power III
d. Program evaluation and review technique

19. _____ is systematic determination of merit, worth, and significance of something or someone using criteria against a set of standards. _____ often is used to characterize and appraise subjects of interest in a wide range of human enterprises, including the arts, criminal justice, foundations and non-profit organizations, government, health care, and other human services.

Depending on the topic of interest, there are professional groups which look to the quality and rigor of the _____ process.

a. ACNielsen
b. ADTECH
c. AMAX
d. Evaluation

20. _____ is defined by the American _____ Association as the activity, set of institutions, and processes for creating, communicating, delivering, and exchanging offerings that have value for customers, clients, partners, and society at large. The term developed from the original meaning which referred literally to going to market, as in shopping, or going to a market to sell goods or services.

_____ practice tends to be seen as a creative industry, which includes advertising, distribution and selling.

a. Gatefold
b. Business marketing
c. Marketing
d. Product naming

21. Consumer market research is a form of applied sociology that concentrates on understanding the behaviours, whims and preferences, of consumers in a market-based economy, and aims to understand the effects and comparative success of marketing campaigns. The field of consumer _____ as a statistical science was pioneered by Arthur Nielsen with the founding of the ACNielsen Company in 1923.

Thus _____ is the systematic and objective identification, collection, analysis, and dissemination of information for the purpose of assisting management in decision making related to the identification and solution of problems and opportunities in marketing.

a. Logit analysis
b. Simple random sampling
c. Market analysis
d. Marketing research

22. The _____ is the major entity that is being analyzed in the study. It is the 'what' or 'whom' that is being studied. In social science research, the most typical units of analysis are individual people.
a. ADTECH
b. AMAX
c. ACNielsen
d. Unit of analysis

23. In statistics, _____ or estimation error is the error caused by observing a sample instead of the whole population.

An estimate of a quantity of interest, such as an average or percentage, will generally be subject to sample-to-sample variation. These variations in the possible sample values of a statistic can theoretically be expressed as _____s, although in practice the exact _____ is typically unknown.

a. Two-tailed test
b. Varimax rotation
c. Power III
d. Sampling error

Chapter 4. Research Design and Implementation

24. A _____ is an error that occurs when a person performs an action on an object that is not the object intended. This error can be very disorienting and usually causes a brief loss of situation awareness or automation surprise if noticed right away. But much worse, if it goes unnoticed, it could cause more serious problems.
   a. Motivation
   b. 180SearchAssistant
   c. Power III
   d. Description error

25. A _____ is an explicit set of requirements to be satisfied by a material, product, or service.

In engineering, manufacturing, and business, it is vital for suppliers, purchasers, and users of materials, products, or services to understand and agree upon all requirements. A _____ is a type of a standard which is often referenced by a contract or procurement document.

   a. New product screening
   b. Specification
   c. Specification tree
   d. Product development

26. _____ is a process of gathering, modeling, and transforming data with the goal of highlighting useful information, suggesting conclusions, and supporting decision making. _____ has multiple facets and approaches, encompassing diverse techniques under a variety of names, in different business, science, and social science domains.

Data mining is a particular _____ technique that focuses on modeling and knowledge discovery for predictive rather than purely descriptive purposes.

   a. Data analysis
   b. 6-3-5 Brainwriting
   c. Power III
   d. 180SearchAssistant

27. _____ is the difference between a measured value of quantity and its true value. In statistics, an error is not a 'mistake'. Variability is an inherent part of things being measured and of the measurement process.
   a. AMAX
   b. ACNielsen
   c. Observational error
   d. ADTECH

Chapter 4. Research Design and Implementation

28. _____ denotes a necessary relationship between one event and another event (called effect) which is the direct consequence of the first.

While this informal understanding suffices in everyday use, the philosophical analysis of how best to characterize _____ extends over millennia. In the western philosophical tradition explicit discussion stretches back at least as far as Aristotle, and the topic remains a staple in contemporary philosophy journals.

   a. 180SearchAssistant
   b. 6-3-5 Brainwriting
   c. Power III
   d. Causality

29. _____ is the validity of (causal) inferences in scientific studies, usually based on experiments as experimental validity .

Inferences are said to possess _____ if a causal relation between two variables is properly demonstrated . A causal inference may be based on a relation when three criteria are satisfied:

   1. the 'cause' precedes the 'effect' in time (temporal precedence),
   2. the 'cause' and the 'effect' are related (covariation), and
   3. there are no plausible alternative explanations for the observed covariation (nonspuriousness) .

In scientific experimental settings, researchers often manipulate a variable (the independent variable) to see what effect it has on a second variable (the dependent variable) For example, a researcher might, for different experimental groups, manipulate the dosage of a particular drug between groups to see what effect it has on health. In this example, the researcher wants to make a causal inference, namely, that different doses of the drug may be held responsible for observed changes or differences.

   a. AMAX
   b. ADTECH
   c. ACNielsen
   d. Internal validity

30. In economics, an externality or spillover of an economic transaction is an impact on a party that is not directly involved in the transaction. In such a case, prices do not reflect the full costs or benefits in production or consumption of a product or service. A positive impact is called an _____ benefit, while a negative impact is called an _____ cost.

a. ACNielsen
b. ADTECH
c. AMAX
d. External

31. _____ is the validity of generalized (causal) inferences in scientific studies, usually based on experiments as experimental validity.

Inferences about cause-effect relationships based on a specific scientific study are said to possess _____ if they may be generalized from the unique and idiosyncratic settings, procedures and participants to other populations and conditions Causal inferences said to possess high degrees of _____ can reasonably be expected to apply (a) to the target population of the study (i.e. from which the sample was drawn) (also referred to as population validity), and (b) to the universe of other populations (e.g. across time and space.)

The most common loss of _____ comes from the fact that experiments using human participants often employ small samples obtained from a single geographic location or with idiosyncratic features (e.g. volunteers.)

a. AMAX
b. External validity
c. ACNielsen
d. ADTECH

Chapter 5. Secondary and Standardized Sources of Marketing Data

1. _____ refer to a collection of facts usually collected as the result of experience, observation or experiment or a set of premises. This may consist of numbers, words particularly as measurements or observations of a set of variables. _____ are often viewed as a lowest level of abstraction from which information and knowledge are derived.
   a. Randomization
   b. Data
   c. Median
   d. P-Value

2. _____ is a term used to describe a process of preparing and collecting data - for example as part of a process improvement or similar project.

   _____ usually takes place early on in an improvement project, and is often formalised through a _____ Plan which often contains the following activity.

   1. Pre collection activity - Agree goals, target data, definitions, methods
   2. Collection - _____
   3. Present Findings - usually involves some form of sorting analysis and/or presentation.

   A formal _____ process is necessary as it ensures that data gathered is both defined and accurate and that subsequent decisions based on arguments embodied in the findings are valid . The process provides both a baseline from which to measure from and in certain cases a target on what to improve. Types of _____ 1-By mail questionnaires 2-By personal interview

   - Six sigma
   - Sampling (statistics)

   a. 6-3-5 Brainwriting
   b. Data collection
   c. Power III
   d. 180SearchAssistant

3. Combining Existing _____ Sources with New Primary Data Sources

Imagine that we could get hold of a good collection of surveys taken in earlier years, such as detailed studies about changes going on in this phase and hopefully additional studies in the years to come. Analyzing this data base over time could give us a good picture of what changes actually have taken place in the orientation of the population and of the extent to which new technical concepts did have an impact on subgroups of the population. Furthermore, data archives can help to prepare studies on change over time by monitoring what questions have been asked in earlier years and alerting principal investigators to important questions which should be repeated in planned research projects.

Chapter 5. Secondary and Standardized Sources of Marketing Data

   a. 6-3-5 Brainwriting
   b. Power III
   c. 180SearchAssistant
   d. Secondary data

4. _____ is a term for unprocessed data, it is also known as primary data. It is a relative term _____ can be input to a computer program or used in manual analysis procedures such as gathering statistics from a survey.
   a. Chief marketing officer
   b. Product manager
   c. Shoppers Food ' Pharmacy
   d. Raw data

5. _____ describes the situation when output from (or information about the result of) an event or phenomenon in the past will influence the same event/phenomenon in the present or future. When an event is part of a chain of cause-and-effect that forms a circuit or loop, then the event is said to 'feed back' into itself.

   _____ is also a synonym for:

   - _____ Signal; the information about the initial event that is the basis for subsequent modification of the event.
   - _____ Loop; the causal path that leads from the initial generation of the _____ signal to the subsequent modification of the event.

   _____ is a mechanism, process or signal that is looped back to control a system within itself. Such a loop is called a _____ loop.

   a. Feedback
   b. Power III
   c. 6-3-5 Brainwriting
   d. 180SearchAssistant

6. A _____ is a structured collection of records or data that is stored in a computer system. The structure is achieved by organizing the data according to a _____ model. The model in most common use today is the relational model.
   a. Database
   b. 6-3-5 Brainwriting
   c. Power III
   d. 180SearchAssistant

Chapter 5. Secondary and Standardized Sources of Marketing Data

7. In economics, an externality or spillover of an economic transaction is an impact on a party that is not directly involved in the transaction. In such a case, prices do not reflect the full costs or benefits in production or consumption of a product or service. A positive impact is called an _____ benefit, while a negative impact is called an _____ cost.
    a. External
    b. ACNielsen
    c. ADTECH
    d. AMAX

8. _____ is defined by the American _____ Association as the activity, set of institutions, and processes for creating, communicating, delivering, and exchanging offerings that have value for customers, clients, partners, and society at large. The term developed from the original meaning which referred literally to going to market, as in shopping, or going to a market to sell goods or services.

    _____ practice tends to be seen as a creative industry, which includes advertising, distribution and selling.

    a. Marketing
    b. Product naming
    c. Business marketing
    d. Gatefold

9. Consumer market research is a form of applied sociology that concentrates on understanding the behaviours, whims and preferences, of consumers in a market-based economy, and aims to understand the effects and comparative success of marketing campaigns. The field of consumer _____ as a statistical science was pioneered by Arthur Nielsen with the founding of the ACNielsen Company in 1923.

    Thus _____ is the systematic and objective identification, collection, analysis, and dissemination of information for the purpose of assisting management in decision making related to the identification and solution of problems and opportunities in marketing.

    a. Simple random sampling
    b. Market analysis
    c. Logit analysis
    d. Marketing research

10. A bibliographic or library database is a database of bibliographic records. It may be a database containing information about books and other materials held in a library (e.g. an online library catalog, or OPAC) or, as the term is more often used, an electronic index to journal or magazine articles, containing citations, abstracts and often either the full text of the articles indexed, or links to the full text.

    Many scientific databases are _____, but some are not.

a. Power III
b. 6-3-5 Brainwriting
c. Bibliographic databases
d. 180SearchAssistant

11. _____s is the social science that studies the production, distribution, and consumption of goods and services. The term _____s comes from the Ancient Greek οἰκονομία from οἶκος (oikos, 'house') + νόμος (nomos, 'custom' or 'law'), hence 'rules of the house(hold)'. Current _____ models developed out of the broader field of political economy in the late 19th century, owing to a desire to use an empirical approach more akin to the physical sciences.
 a. ACNielsen
 b. Industrial organization
 c. ADTECH
 d. Economic

12. _____ is the study of the Earth and its lands, features, inhabitants, and phenomena. A literal translation would be 'to describe or write about the Earth'. The first person to use the word '_____' was Eratosthenes.
 a. Geography
 b. Power III
 c. 180SearchAssistant
 d. 6-3-5 Brainwriting

13. In the United States, the Office of Management and Budget (OMB) has produced a formal definition of metropolitan areas. These are referred to as '_____s' (_____s) and 'Combined Statistical Areas.' An earlier version of the _____ was the 'Standard _____' (SMetropolitan statistical area.) _____s are composed of counties and for some county equivalents.
 a. Metropolitan statistical area
 b. Race and ethnicity in the United States Census
 c. 180SearchAssistant
 d. Power III

14. An _____ is the manufacturing of a good or service within a category. Although _____ is a broad term for any kind of economic production, in economics and urban planning _____ is a synonym for the secondary sector, which is a type of economic activity involved in the manufacturing of raw materials into goods and products.

Chapter 5. Secondary and Standardized Sources of Marketing Data 31

There are four key industrial economic sectors: the primary sector, largely raw material extraction industries such as mining and farming; the secondary sector, involving refining, construction, and manufacturing; the tertiary sector, which deals with services (such as law and medicine) and distribution of manufactured goods; and the quaternary sector, a relatively new type of knowledge _____ focusing on technological research, design and development such as computer programming, and biochemistry.

  a. AMAX
  b. ACNielsen
  c. Industry
  d. ADTECH

15. The _____ or _____ is used by business and government to classify and measure economic activity in Canada, Mexico and the United States. It has largely replaced the older Standard Industrial Classification system; however, certain government departments and agencies, such as the U.S. Securities and Exchange Commission (SEC), still use the SIC codes.

The _____ numbering system is a six-digit code.

  a. North American Industry Classification System
  b. Power III
  c. 6-3-5 Brainwriting
  d. 180SearchAssistant

16. In economics, _____ is the desire to own something and the ability to pay for it. The term _____ signifies the ability or the willingness to buy a particular commodity at a given point of time .

  a. Market dominance
  b. Discretionary spending
  c. Demand
  d. Market system

17. _____ is the process of finding associated geographic coordinates (often expressed as latitude and longitude) from other geographic data, such as street addresses or the coordinates can be embedded into media such as digital photographs via geotagging.

Reverse _____ is the opposite: finding an associated textual location such as a street address, from geographic coordinates.

Chapter 5. Secondary and Standardized Sources of Marketing Data

a. 180SearchAssistant
b. Power III
c. 6-3-5 Brainwriting
d. Geocoding

18. _____ is an advertisement in which a particular product specifically mentions a competitor by name for the express purpose of showing why the competitor is inferior to the product naming it.

This should not be confused with parody advertisements, where a fictional product is being advertised for the purpose of poking fun at the particular advertisement, nor should it be confused with the use of a coined brand name for the purpose of comparing the product without actually naming an actual competitor. ('Wikipedia tastes better and is less filling than the Encyclopedia Galactica.')

In the 1980s, during what has been referred to as the cola wars, soft-drink manufacturer Pepsi ran a series of advertisements where people, caught on hidden camera, in a blind taste test, chose Pepsi over rival Coca-Cola.

a. GL-70
b. Comparative advertising
c. Heavy-up
d. Cost per conversion

19. The United States _____ is the Cabinet department of the United States government concerned with promoting economic growth. It was originally created as the United States _____ and Labor on February 14, 1903. It was subsequently renamed to the _____ on March 4, 1913, and its bureaus and agencies specializing in labor were transferred to the new Department of Labor.
a. Power III
b. 6-3-5 Brainwriting
c. 180SearchAssistant
d. Department of Commerce

20. The _____ is the Cabinet department of the United States government concerned with promoting economic growth. It was originally created as the _____ and Labor on February 14, 1903. It was subsequently renamed to the Department of Commerce on March 4, 1913, and its bureaus and agencies specializing in labor were transferred to the new Department of Labor.
a. ACNielsen
b. ADTECH
c. AMAX
d. United States Department of Commerce

Chapter 5. Secondary and Standardized Sources of Marketing Data 33

21. The _____ is an international organization whose stated aims are to facilitate cooperation in international law, international security, economic development, social progress, human rights and achieving world peace. The _____ was founded in 1945 after World War II to replace the League of Nations, to stop wars between countries and to provide a platform for dialogue.

There are currently 192 member states, including nearly every recognized independent state in the world.

 a. United Nations
 b. ACNielsen
 c. AMAX
 d. ADTECH

22. The _____ is an international financial institution that provides financial and technical assistance to developing countries for development programs (e.g. bridges, roads, schools, etc.) with the stated goal of reducing poverty.

The _____ differs from the _____ Group, in that the _____ comprises only two institutions:

- International Bank for Reconstruction and Development (IBRD)
- International Development Association (IDA)

Whereas the latter incorporates these two in addition to three more:

- International Finance Corporation (IFC)
- Multilateral Investment Guarantee Agency (MIGA)
- International Centre for Settlement of Investment Disputes (ICSID)

John Maynard Keynes (right) represented the UK at the conference, and Harry Dexter White represented the US.

The _____ was created following the ratification of the United Nations Monetary and Financial Conference of the Bretton Woods agreement. The concept was originally conceived in July 1944 at the United Nations Monetary and Financial Conference.

 a. Power III
 b. World Bank
 c. 6-3-5 Brainwriting
 d. 180SearchAssistant

23. _____ is the process of estimation in unknown situations. Prediction is a similar, but more general term. Both can refer to estimation of time series, cross-sectional or longitudinal data.

34 *Chapter 5. Secondary and Standardized Sources of Marketing Data*

a. Power III
b. 6-3-5 Brainwriting
c. 180SearchAssistant
d. Forecasting

24. The general definition of an _____ is an evaluation of a person, organization, system, process, project or product. _____s are performed to ascertain the validity and reliability of information; also to provide an assessment of a system's internal control. The goal of an _____ is to express an opinion on the person/organization/system (etc) in question, under evaluation based on work done on a test basis.
    a. AMAX
    b. ADTECH
    c. Audit
    d. ACNielsen

25. _____ is a broad label that refers to any individuals or households that use goods and services generated within the economy. The concept of a _____ is used in different contexts, so that the usage and significance of the term may vary.

A _____ is a person who uses any product or service.

   a. 6-3-5 Brainwriting
   b. Power III
   c. 180SearchAssistant
   d. Consumer

26. _____ often refers to either primary or secondary research. Secondary research involves a company using information compiled from various sources, which is about a new or existing product. The advantages of secondary research are that it is relatively cheap and easily accessible.
    a. Questionnaire
    b. Market Research
    c. Mystery shoppers
    d. Mystery shopping

27. _____ is a standard point of view or personal prejudice. especially when the tendency interferes with the ability to be impartial, unprejudiced, or objective. The term _____ed is used to describe an action, judgment, or other outcome influenced by a prejudged perspective.

Chapter 5. Secondary and Standardized Sources of Marketing Data

a. 180SearchAssistant
b. Bias
c. Power III
d. 6-3-5 Brainwriting

28. _____ is a distortion of evidence or data that arises from the way that the data are collected. It is sometimes referred to as the selection effect. The term _____ most often refers to the distortion of a statistical analysis, due to the method of collecting samples.

   a. Power III
   b. 180SearchAssistant
   c. Selection bias
   d. Systematic sampling

29. Human beings are also considered to be _____ because they have the ability to change raw materials into valuable _____. The term Human _____ can also be defined as the skills, energies, talents, abilities and knowledge that are used for the production of goods or the rendering of services. While taking into account human beings as _____, the following things have to be kept in mind:

   - The size of the population
   - The capabilities of the individuals in that population

Many _____ cannot be consumed in their original form. They have to be processed in order to change them into more usable commodities.

   a. Power III
   b. Resources
   c. 180SearchAssistant
   d. 6-3-5 Brainwriting

30. _____ involves disseminating information about a product, product line, brand, or company. It is one of the four key aspects of the marketing mix. (The other three elements are product marketing, pricing, and distribution). P>_____ is generally sub-divided into two parts:

   - Above the line _____: Promotion in the media (e.g. TV, radio, newspapers, Internet and Mobile Phones) in which the advertiser pays an advertising agency to place the ad
   - Below the line _____: All other _____. Much of this is intended to be subtle enough for the consumer to be unaware that _____ is taking place. E.g. sponsorship, product placement, endorsements, sales _____, merchandising, direct mail, personal selling, public relations, trade shows

Chapter 5. Secondary and Standardized Sources of Marketing Data

a. Technology maturity lifecycle
b. Promotion
c. Cash and carry
d. M80

31. A _____ is a tool used to measure the viewing habits of TV and cable audiences.

The _____ is a 'box', about the size of a paperback book. The box is hooked up to each television set and is accompanied by a remote control unit.

a. Power III
b. 6-3-5 Brainwriting
c. 180SearchAssistant
d. People meter

32. _____ is a radio audience research company in the United States which collects listener data on radio audiences similar to that collected by Nielsen Media Research on television audiences. It was founded as American Research Bureau by Jim Seiler in 1949 and became bi-coastal by merging with L.A. based Coffin, Cooper and Clay in the early 1950s. ARB's initial business was the collection of television broadcast ratings exclusively.
a. American Heart Association
b. American Cancer Society
c. Access Commerce
d. Arbitron

33. _____ is a blanket term used for pre-recorded media that is either sold or hired for home entertainment. The term originates from the VHS/Betamax era but has carried over into the current DVD/Blu-ray Disc age. The first company to duplicate and distribute _____ was Magnetic Video, established in 1968.
a. 180SearchAssistant
b. Home Video
c. 6-3-5 Brainwriting
d. Power III

34. _____ is an American firm that measures media audiences, including television, radio, theatre films (via the AMC MAP program) and newspapers. _____, headquartered in New York City and operating primarily from Chicago, is best-known for the Nielsen Ratings, a measurement of television viewership.

_____, the preeminent media research company in the world, began as a division of ACNielsen, a marketing research firm.

a. Superbrands
b. Coinstar
c. Zany Brainy
d. Nielsen Media Research

Chapter 6. Marketing Research on the Internet

1. _____ is an independent technology and market research company that provides its clients with advice about technology's impact on business and consumers. _____ has four research centers in the US: Cambridge, Massachusetts; Foster City, California; Washington, D.C.; and Westport, Connecticut. It also has four European research centers in Amsterdam, Frankfurt, London, and Paris.
   a. National Asset Recovery Services
   b. Mapinfo
   c. Checkoff
   d. Forrester Research

2. A _____ is a relatively new executive level position at a corporation, company, organization typically reporting directly to the CEO or board of directors. The _____ is responsible for a brand's image, experience, and promise, and propagating it throughout all aspects of the company. The brand officer oversees marketing, advertising, design, public relations and customer service departments.
   a. Decision Analyst
   b. Power III
   c. Chief executive officer
   d. Chief brand officer

3. _____ is a technique used in propaganda and advertising. Also known as association, this is a technique of projecting positive or negative qualities (praise or blame) of a person, entity, object, or value (an individual, group, organization, nation, patriotism, etc.) to another in order to make the second more acceptable or to discredit it.
   a. Per-inquiry advertising
   b. Transfer
   c. Relationship Management Application
   d. Gross Margin Return on Inventory Investment

4. The _____ is a very large set of interlinked hypertext documents accessed via the Internet. With a Web browser, one can view Web pages that may contain text, images, videos, and other multimedia and navigate between them using hyperlinks. Using concepts from earlier hypertext systems, the _____ was begun in 1992 by the English physicist Sir Tim Berners-Lee, now the Director of the _____ Consortium, and Robert Cailliau, a Belgian computer scientist, while both were working at CERN in Geneva, Switzerland.
   a. 6-3-5 Brainwriting
   b. Power III
   c. 180SearchAssistant
   d. World Wide Web

Chapter 6. Marketing Research on the Internet

5. _____ or _____ data refers to selected population characteristics as used in government, marketing or opinion research, or the _____ profiles used in such research. Note the distinction from the term 'demography' Commonly-used _____ include race, age, income, disabilities, mobility (in terms of travel time to work or number of vehicles available), educational attainment, home ownership, employment status, and even location.

   a. AStore
   b. Albert Einstein
   c. Demographic
   d. African Americans

6. _____ is a form of communication that typically attempts to persuade potential customers to purchase or to consume more of a particular brand of product or service. 'While now central to the contemporary global economy and the reproduction of global production networks, it is only quite recently that _____ has been more than a marginal influence on patterns of sales and production. The formation of modern _____ was intimately bound up with the emergence of new forms of monopoly capitalism around the end of the 19th and beginning of the 20th century as one element in corporate strategies to create, organize and where possible control markets, especially for mass produced consumer goods.

   a. Advertising
   b. AMAX
   c. ACNielsen
   d. ADTECH

7. _____ is defined by the American _____ Association as the activity, set of institutions, and processes for creating, communicating, delivering, and exchanging offerings that have value for customers, clients, partners, and society at large. The term developed from the original meaning which referred literally to going to market, as in shopping, or going to a market to sell goods or services.

   _____ practice tends to be seen as a creative industry, which includes advertising, distribution and selling.

   a. Business marketing
   b. Product naming
   c. Gatefold
   d. Marketing

8. _____ is an American firm that measures media audiences, including television, radio, theatre films (via the AMC MAP program) and newspapers. _____, headquartered in New York City and operating primarily from Chicago, is best-known for the Nielsen Ratings, a measurement of television viewership.

   _____, the preeminent media research company in the world, began as a division of ACNielsen, a marketing research firm.

a. Superbrands
b. Coinstar
c. Zany Brainy
d. Nielsen Media Research

9. _____ is a term for unprocessed data, it is also known as primary data. It is a relative term _____ can be input to a computer program or used in manual analysis procedures such as gathering statistics from a survey.

a. Shoppers Food ' Pharmacy
b. Chief marketing officer
c. Product manager
d. Raw data

10. _____ refer to a collection of facts usually collected as the result of experience, observation or experiment or a set of premises. This may consist of numbers, words particularly as measurements or observations of a set of variables. _____ are often viewed as a lowest level of abstraction from which information and knowledge are derived.

a. P-Value
b. Randomization
c. Median
d. Data

11. Consumer market research is a form of applied sociology that concentrates on understanding the behaviours, whims and preferences, of consumers in a market-based economy, and aims to understand the effects and comparative success of marketing campaigns. The field of consumer _____ as a statistical science was pioneered by Arthur Nielsen with the founding of the ACNielsen Company in 1923 .

Thus _____ is the systematic and objective identification, collection, analysis, and dissemination of information for the purpose of assisting management in decision making related to the identification and solution of problems and opportunities in marketing.

a. Logit analysis
b. Marketing research
c. Market analysis
d. Simple random sampling

12. A _____ is a form of qualitative research in which a group of people are asked about their attitude towards a product, service, concept, advertisement, idea, or packaging. Questions are asked in an interactive group setting where participants are free to talk with other group members.

Chapter 6. Marketing Research on the Internet

Ernest Dichter originated the idea of having a 'group therapy' for products and this process is what became known as a _____.

a. Simple random sampling
b. Preference regression
c. Focus group
d. Market analysis

13. _____, also referred to as i-marketing, web marketing, online marketing is the marketing of products or services over the Internet.

The Internet has brought many unique benefits to marketing, one of which being lower costs for the distribution of information and media to a global audience. The interactive nature of _____, both in terms of providing instant response and eliciting responses, is a unique quality of the medium.

a. ACNielsen
b. Internet marketing
c. ADTECH
d. AMAX

14. _____ is an advertisement in which a particular product specifically mentions a competitor by name for the express purpose of showing why the competitor is inferior to the product naming it.

This should not be confused with parody advertisements, where a fictional product is being advertised for the purpose of poking fun at the particular advertisement, nor should it be confused with the use of a coined brand name for the purpose of comparing the product without actually naming an actual competitor. ('Wikipedia tastes better and is less filling than the Encyclopedia Galactica.')

In the 1980s, during what has been referred to as the cola wars, soft-drink manufacturer Pepsi ran a series of advertisements where people, caught on hidden camera, in a blind taste test, chose Pepsi over rival Coca-Cola.

a. Comparative advertising
b. GL-70
c. Heavy-up
d. Cost per conversion

Chapter 6. Marketing Research on the Internet

15. Electronic commerce, commonly known as _____ or eCommerce, consists of the buying and selling of products or services over electronic systems such as the Internet and other computer networks. The amount of trade conducted electronically has grown extraordinarily with wide-spread Internet usage. A wide variety of commerce is conducted in this way, spurring and drawing on innovations in electronic funds transfer, supply chain management, Internet marketing, online transaction processing, electronic data interchange (EDI), inventory management systems, and automated data collection systems.

   a. ADTECH
   b. ACNielsen
   c. AMAX
   d. E-commerce

16. _____ is a branch of philosophy which seeks to address questions about morality, such as how a moral outcome can be achieved in a specific situation (applied _____), how moral values should be determined (normative _____), what moral values people actually abide by (descriptive _____), what the fundamental semantic, ontological, and epistemic nature of _____ or morality is (meta-_____), and how moral capacity or moral agency develops and what its nature is (moral psychology.)

Socrates was one of the first Greek philosophers to encourage both scholars and the common citizen to turn their attention from the outside world to the condition of man. In this view, Knowledge having a bearing on human life was placed highest, all other knowledge being secondary.

   a. Ethics
   b. ACNielsen
   c. AMAX
   d. ADTECH

17. _____, commonly known as e-commerce or eCommerce, consists of the buying and selling of products or services over electronic systems such as the Internet and other computer networks. The amount of trade conducted electronically has grown extraordinarily with wide-spread Internet usage. A wide variety of commerce is conducted in this way, spurring and drawing on innovations in electronic funds transfer, supply chain management, Internet marketing, online transaction processing, electronic data interchange (EDI), inventory management systems, and automated data collection systems.

   a. AMAX
   b. ADTECH
   c. Electronic Commerce
   d. ACNielsen

18. The term _____ refers to several methods by which individuals can avoid receiving unsolicited product or service information. This ability is usually associated with direct marketing campaigns such as telemarketing, e-mail marketing, or direct mail.

Chapter 6. Marketing Research on the Internet

The U.S. Federal Government created the National Do Not Call Registry to reduce the telemarketing calls consumers receive at home.

a. Opt-out
b. ACNielsen
c. AMAX
d. ADTECH

19. _____ LLP, based in Chicago, was once one of the 'Big Five' accounting firms among PricewaterhouseCoopers, Deloitte Touche Tohmatsu, Ernst ' Young and KPMG, providing auditing, tax, and consulting services to large corporations. In 2002, the firm voluntarily surrendered its licenses to practice as Certified Public Accountants in the United States after being found guilty of criminal charges relating to the firm's handling of the auditing of Enron, the energy corporation, resulting in the loss of 85,000 jobs. Although the verdict was subsequently overturned by the Supreme Court of the United States, it has not returned as a viable business.
   a. Arthur Andersen
   b. ACNielsen
   c. AMAX
   d. ADTECH

20. An _____ is a private network that uses Internet protocols, network connectivity, and possibly the public telecommunication system to securely share part of an organization's information or operations with suppliers, vendors, partners, customers or other businesses. An _____ can be viewed as part of a company's intranet that is extended to users outside the company (e.g.: normally over the Internet.) It has also been described as a 'state of mind' in which the Internet is perceived as a way to do business with a preapproved set of other companies business-to-business (B2B), in isolation from all other Internet users.
   a. ADTECH
   b. ACNielsen
   c. AMAX
   d. Extranet

21. _____ is the pioneer of the digital video recorder . _____ was introduced in the United States, and is now available in Canada, Mexico, Australia, and Taiwan. Created by _____, Inc..
   a. 6-3-5 Brainwriting
   b. TiVo
   c. Power III
   d. 180SearchAssistant

Chapter 7. Information Collection: Qualitative and Observational Methods

1. _____ refer to a collection of facts usually collected as the result of experience, observation or experiment or a set of premises. This may consist of numbers, words particularly as measurements or observations of a set of variables. _____ are often viewed as a lowest level of abstraction from which information and knowledge are derived.
   a. Median
   b. Data
   c. Randomization
   d. P-Value

2. _____ is a term used to describe a process of preparing and collecting data - for example as part of a process improvement or similar project.

   _____ usually takes place early on in an improvement project, and is often formalised through a _____ Plan which often contains the following activity.

   1. Pre collection activity - Agree goals, target data, definitions, methods
   2. Collection - _____
   3. Present Findings - usually involves some form of sorting analysis and/or presentation.

   A formal _____ process is necessary as it ensures that data gathered is both defined and accurate and that subsequent decisions based on arguments embodied in the findings are valid . The process provides both a baseline from which to measure from and in certain cases a target on what to improve. Types of _____ 1-By mail questionnaires 2-By personal interview

   - Six sigma
   - Sampling (statistics)

   a. Data collection
   b. Power III
   c. 180SearchAssistant
   d. 6-3-5 Brainwriting

3. _____ is a field of inquiry that crosscuts disciplines and subject matters . _____ers aim to gather an in-depth understanding of human behavior and the reasons that govern such behavior. The discipline investigates the why and how of decision making, not just what, where, when.
   a. Power III
   b. 180SearchAssistant
   c. 6-3-5 Brainwriting
   d. Qualitative research

Chapter 7. Information Collection: Qualitative and Observational Methods

4. Electronic commerce, commonly known as _____ or eCommerce, consists of the buying and selling of products or services over electronic systems such as the Internet and other computer networks. The amount of trade conducted electronically has grown extraordinarily with wide-spread Internet usage. A wide variety of commerce is conducted in this way, spurring and drawing on innovations in electronic funds transfer, supply chain management, Internet marketing, online transaction processing, electronic data interchange (EDI), inventory management systems, and automated data collection systems.

   a. ADTECH
   b. AMAX
   c. ACNielsen
   d. E-commerce

5. _____ is an investment technique that requires investors to purchase multiple financial products with different maturity dates.

   _____ avoids the risk of reinvesting a big portion of assets in an unfavorable financial environment. For example, a person has both a 2015 matured CD and a 2018 matured CD.

   a. Power III
   b. Laddering
   c. 180SearchAssistant
   d. 6-3-5 Brainwriting

6. _____ is a metatheory, which is used for interpreting relations between symbols. It can be made either manually or by using computer tools.

   All languages are made up of symbols.

   a. Graphic communication
   b. Symbolic analysis
   c. Public relations
   d. Power III

7. _____ in organizations and public policy is both the organizational process of creating and maintaining a plan; and the psychological process of thinking about the activities required to create a desired goal on some scale. As such, it is a fundamental property of intelligent behavior. This thought process is essential to the creation and refinement of a plan, or integration of it with other plans, that is, it combines forecasting of developments with the preparation of scenarios of how to react to them.

a. Power III
b. 6-3-5 Brainwriting
c. 180SearchAssistant
d. Planning

8. A _____ is a form of qualitative research in which a group of people are asked about their attitude towards a product, service, concept, advertisement, idea, or packaging. Questions are asked in an interactive group setting where participants are free to talk with other group members.

Ernest Dichter originated the idea of having a 'group therapy' for products and this process is what became known as a _____.

a. Preference regression
b. Market analysis
c. Simple random sampling
d. Focus group

9. _____ generally refers to a list of all planned expenses and revenues. It is a plan for saving and spending. A _____ is an important concept in microeconomics, which uses a _____ line to illustrate the trade-offs between two or more goods.
a. Budget
b. 6-3-5 Brainwriting
c. Power III
d. 180SearchAssistant

10. In economics, business, retail, and accounting, a _____ is the value of money that has been used up to produce something, and hence is not available for use anymore. In economics, a _____ is an alternative that is given up as a result of a decision. In business, the _____ may be one of acquisition, in which case the amount of money expended to acquire it is counted as _____.
a. Transaction cost
b. Cost
c. Fixed costs
d. Marginal cost

11. _____ is a common word game involving an exchange of words that are associated together.

Chapter 7. Information Collection: Qualitative and Observational Methods   47

Once an original word has been chosen, usually randomly or arbitrarily, a player will find a word that they associate with it and make it known to all the players, usually by saying it aloud or writing it down as the next item on a list of words so far used. The next player must then do the same with this previous word.

  a. Power III
  b. Word association
  c. 6-3-5 Brainwriting
  d. 180SearchAssistant

12. The _____ is an example of a projective test.

Historically, the _____ or _____ has been amongst the most widely used, researched, and taught projective psychological tests. Its adherents claim that it taps a subject's unconscious to reveal repressed aspects of personality, motives and needs for achievement, power and intimacy, and problem-solving abilities.

  a. Thematic Apperception Test
  b. 180SearchAssistant
  c. Power III
  d. 6-3-5 Brainwriting

13. _____ is a form of communication that typically attempts to persuade potential customers to purchase or to consume more of a particular brand of product or service. 'While now central to the contemporary global economy and the reproduction of global production networks, it is only quite recently that _____ has been more than a marginal influence on patterns of sales and production. The formation of modern _____ was intimately bound up with the emergence of new forms of monopoly capitalism around the end of the 19th and beginning of the 20th century as one element in corporate strategies to create, organize and where possible control markets, especially for mass produced consumer goods.
  a. Advertising
  b. AMAX
  c. ADTECH
  d. ACNielsen

14. _____ is a type of research conducted because a problem has not been clearly defined. _____ helps determine the best research design, data collection method and selection of subjects. Given its fundamental nature, _____ often concludes that a perceived problem does not actually exist.

Chapter 7. Information Collection: Qualitative and Observational Methods

a. Intent scale translation
b. IDDEA
c. ACNielsen
d. Exploratory research

15. _____ is a standard point of view or personal prejudice. especially when the tendency interferes with the ability to be impartial, unprejudiced, or objective. The term _____ed is used to describe an action, judgment, or other outcome influenced by a prejudged perspective.

a. 180SearchAssistant
b. Power III
c. Bias
d. 6-3-5 Brainwriting

16. A _____ is a diagram used to represent words, ideas, tasks, or other items linked to and arranged around a central key word or idea. _____s are used to generate, visualize, structure, and classify ideas, and as an aid in study, organization, problem solving, decision making, and writing.

The elements of a given _____ are arranged intuitively according to the importance of the concepts, and are classified into groupings, branches, or areas, with the goal of representing semantic or other connections between portions of information.

a. 6-3-5 Brainwriting
b. Mind map
c. Power III
d. 180SearchAssistant

17. _____ is either an activity of a living being (such as a human), consisting of receiving knowledge of the outside world through the senses, or the recording of data using scientific instruments. The term may also refer to any datum collected during this activity.

The scientific method requires _____s of nature to formulate and test hypotheses.

a. Observation
b. ACNielsen
c. ADTECH
d. AMAX

Chapter 7. Information Collection: Qualitative and Observational Methods 49

18. _____ is a methodology in the social sciences for studying the content of communication. Earl Babbie defines it as 'the study of recorded human communications, such as books, websites, paintings and laws.' It is most commonly used by researchers in the social sciences to analyze recorded transcripts of interviews with participants.

_____ is also considered a scholarly methodology in the humanities by which texts are studied as to authorship, authenticity, of meaning.

   a. Power III
   b. 180SearchAssistant
   c. Content analysis
   d. 6-3-5 Brainwriting

19. The general definition of an _____ is an evaluation of a person, organization, system, process, project or product. _____s are performed to ascertain the validity and reliability of information; also to provide an assessment of a system's internal control. The goal of an _____ is to express an opinion on the person/organization/system (etc) in question, under evaluation based on work done on a test basis.
   a. ADTECH
   b. AMAX
   c. ACNielsen
   d. Audit

20. _____ is a radio audience research company in the United States which collects listener data on radio audiences similar to that collected by Nielsen Media Research on television audiences. It was founded as American Research Bureau by Jim Seiler in 1949 and became bi-coastal by merging with L.A. based Coffin, Cooper and Clay in the early 1950s. ARB's initial business was the collection of television broadcast ratings exclusively.
   a. American Heart Association
   b. Access Commerce
   c. American Cancer Society
   d. Arbitron

21. In probability theory and statistics, _____ indicates the strength and direction of a linear relationship between two random variables. That is in contrast with the usage of the term in colloquial speech, denoting any relationship, not necessarily linear. In general statistical usage, _____ or co-relation refers to the departure of two random variables from independence.
   a. Stratified sampling
   b. Type I error
   c. Correlation
   d. Standard normal distribution

Chapter 7. Information Collection: Qualitative and Observational Methods

22. A _____ is a tool used to measure the viewing habits of TV and cable audiences.

The _____ is a 'box', about the size of a paperback book. The box is hooked up to each television set and is accompanied by a remote control unit.

   a. Power III
   b. 180SearchAssistant
   c. 6-3-5 Brainwriting
   d. People meter

23. In statistics, _____ is a collective name for techniques for the modeling and analysis of numerical data consisting of values of a dependent variable and of one or more independent variables The dependent variable in the regression equation is modeled as a function of the independent variables, corresponding parameters, and an error term. The error term is treated as a random variable.
   a. Variance inflation factor
   b. Multicollinearity
   c. Stepwise regression
   d. Regression analysis

Chapter 8. Information from Respondents: Issues in Data Collection

1. _____ refer to a collection of facts usually collected as the result of experience, observation or experiment or a set of premises. This may consist of numbers, words particularly as measurements or observations of a set of variables. _____ are often viewed as a lowest level of abstraction from which information and knowledge are derived.
   a. P-Value
   b. Median
   c. Randomization
   d. Data

2. _____ is a term used to describe a process of preparing and collecting data - for example as part of a process improvement or similar project.

_____ usually takes place early on in an improvement project, and is often formalised through a _____ Plan which often contains the following activity.

   1. Pre collection activity - Agree goals, target data, definitions, methods
   2. Collection - _____
   3. Present Findings - usually involves some form of sorting analysis and/or presentation.

A formal _____ process is necessary as it ensures that data gathered is both defined and accurate and that subsequent decisions based on arguments embodied in the findings are valid . The process provides both a baseline from which to measure from and in certain cases a target on what to improve. Types of _____ 1-By mail questionnaires 2-By personal interview

   - Six sigma
   - Sampling (statistics)

   a. 180SearchAssistant
   b. 6-3-5 Brainwriting
   c. Data collection
   d. Power III

3. _____ is defined by the American _____ Association as the activity, set of institutions, and processes for creating, communicating, delivering, and exchanging offerings that have value for customers, clients, partners, and society at large. The term developed from the original meaning which referred literally to going to market, as in shopping, or going to a market to sell goods or services.

_____ practice tends to be seen as a creative industry, which includes advertising, distribution and selling.

Chapter 8. Information from Respondents: Issues in Data Collection

a. Product naming
b. Business marketing
c. Gatefold
d. Marketing

4. _____ , according to Cornish, 'the process of acquiring and analyzing information in order to understand the market (both existing and potential customers); to determine the current and future needs and preferences, attitudes and behavior of the market; and to assess changes in the business environment that may affect the size and nature of the market in the future.' ('Product', 1997, p147.)

This figure shows how the interaction between variables from producers, communication channels, and consumers vary the effectiveness of _____ which affects the performance of the sales of a new product. The product is central in a circle because it helps to direct what information is gathered and how.

a. Specialty catalogs
b. Co-branding
c. Brand parity
d. Market intelligence

5. A _____ is a research instrument consisting of a series of questions and other prompts for the purpose of gathering information from respondents. Although they are often designed for statistical analysis of the responses, this is not always the case. The _____ was invented by Sir Francis Galton.

a. Mystery shoppers
b. Mystery shopping
c. Questionnaire
d. Market research

6. Consumer market research is a form of applied sociology that concentrates on understanding the behaviours, whims and preferences, of consumers in a market-based economy, and aims to understand the effects and comparative success of marketing campaigns. The field of consumer _____ as a statistical science was pioneered by Arthur Nielsen with the founding of the ACNielsen Company in 1923 .

Thus _____ is the systematic and objective identification, collection, analysis, and dissemination of information for the purpose of assisting management in decision making related to the identification and solution of problems and opportunities in marketing.

a. Logit analysis
b. Market analysis
c. Marketing research
d. Simple random sampling

7. _____ is a standard point of view or personal prejudice. especially when the tendency interferes with the ability to be impartial, unprejudiced, or objective. The term _____ed is used to describe an action, judgment, or other outcome influenced by a prejudged perspective.
   a. Bias
   b. Power III
   c. 6-3-5 Brainwriting
   d. 180SearchAssistant

8. _____ is a type of cognitive bias which can affect the results of a statistical survey if respondents answer questions in the way they think the questioner wants them to answer rather than according to their true beliefs. This may occur if the questioner is obviously angling for a particular answer (as in push polling) or if the respondent wishes to please the questioner by answering what appears to be the 'morally right' answer. An example of the latter might be if a woman surveys a man on his attitudes to domestic violence, or someone who obviously cares about the environment asks people how much they value a wilderness area.
   a. Von Restorff effect
   b. Power III
   c. 180SearchAssistant
   d. Response bias

9. An _____ is the manufacturing of a good or service within a category. Although _____ is a broad term for any kind of economic production, in economics and urban planning _____ is a synonym for the secondary sector, which is a type of economic activity involved in the manufacturing of raw materials into goods and products.

There are four key industrial economic sectors: the primary sector, largely raw material extraction industries such as mining and farming; the secondary sector, involving refining, construction, and manufacturing; the tertiary sector, which deals with services (such as law and medicine) and distribution of manufactured goods; and the quaternary sector, a relatively new type of knowledge _____ focusing on technological research, design and development such as computer programming, and biochemistry.

   a. ACNielsen
   b. ADTECH
   c. AMAX
   d. Industry

10. Electronic commerce, commonly known as _____ or eCommerce, consists of the buying and selling of products or services over electronic systems such as the Internet and other computer networks. The amount of trade conducted electronically has grown extraordinarily with wide-spread Internet usage. A wide variety of commerce is conducted in this way, spurring and drawing on innovations in electronic funds transfer, supply chain management, Internet marketing, online transaction processing, electronic data interchange (EDI), inventory management systems, and automated data collection systems.
   a. ADTECH
   b. ACNielsen
   c. AMAX
   d. E-commerce

11. _____ is a field of inquiry that crosscuts disciplines and subject matters . _____ers aim to gather an in-depth understanding of human behavior and the reasons that govern such behavior. The discipline investigates the why and how of decision making, not just what, where, when.
   a. 180SearchAssistant
   b. Power III
   c. 6-3-5 Brainwriting
   d. Qualitative research

12. _____ a research method involving the use of questionnaires and/or statistical surveys to gather data about people and their thoughts and behaviours.
   a. Randomization
   b. Control chart
   c. Stratified sampling
   d. Survey research

13. _____ is a sales technique in which a salesperson walks from one door of a house to another trying to sell a product or service to the general public. A variant of this involves cold calling first, when another sales representative attempts to gain agreement that a salesperson should visit. _____ selling is usually conducted in the afternoon hours, when the majority of people are at home.
   a. Marketing management
   b. Business structure
   c. Fast moving consumer goods
   d. Door-to-door

Chapter 8. Information from Respondents: Issues in Data Collection 55

14. _____ is the conveying of events in words, images, and sounds often by improvisation or embellishment. Stories or narratives have been shared in every culture and in every land as a means of entertainment, education, preservation of culture and in order to instill moral values. Crucial elements of stories and _____ include plot and characters, as well as the narrative point of view.
   a. Power III
   b. 180SearchAssistant
   c. 6-3-5 Brainwriting
   d. Storytelling

15. _____ is an advertisement in which a particular product specifically mentions a competitor by name for the express purpose of showing why the competitor is inferior to the product naming it.

This should not be confused with parody advertisements, where a fictional product is being advertised for the purpose of poking fun at the particular advertisement, nor should it be confused with the use of a coined brand name for the purpose of comparing the product without actually naming an actual competitor. ('Wikipedia tastes better and is less filling than the Encyclopedia Galactica.')

In the 1980s, during what has been referred to as the cola wars, soft-drink manufacturer Pepsi ran a series of advertisements where people, caught on hidden camera, in a blind taste test, chose Pepsi over rival Coca-Cola.

   a. Comparative advertising
   b. Heavy-up
   c. GL-70
   d. Cost per conversion

16. Combining Existing _____ Sources with New Primary Data Sources

Imagine that we could get hold of a good collection of surveys taken in earlier years, such as detailed studies about changes going on in this phase and hopefully additional studies in the years to come. Analyzing this data base over time could give us a good picture of what changes actually have taken place in the orientation of the population and of the extent to which new technical concepts did have an impact on subgroups of the population. Furthermore, data archives can help to prepare studies on change over time by monitoring what questions have been asked in earlier years and alerting principal investigators to important questions which should be repeated in planned research projects.

   a. 180SearchAssistant
   b. 6-3-5 Brainwriting
   c. Power III
   d. Secondary data

Chapter 8. Information from Respondents: Issues in Data Collection

17. _____ is the practice of individuals including commercial businesses, governments and institutions, facilitating the sale of their products or services to other companies or organizations that in turn resell them, use them as components in products or services they offer _____ is also called business-to-_____ for short. (Note that while marketing to government entities shares some of the same dynamics of organizational marketing, B2G Marketing is meaningfully different.)

   a. Customer franchise
   b. Marketspace
   c. Business marketing
   d. Buy one, get one free

18. _____ in survey research refers to the ratio of number of people who answered the survey divided by the number of people in the sample. It is usually expressed in the form of a percentage.

   Example: if 1,000 surveys were sent by mail, and 257 were successfully completed and returned, then the _____ would be 25.7 %.

   a. Sentence completion tests
   b. Power III
   c. Reference value
   d. Response rate

19. _____ is a branch of philosophy which seeks to address questions about morality, such as how a moral outcome can be achieved in a specific situation (applied _____), how moral values should be determined (normative _____), what moral values people actually abide by (descriptive _____), what the fundamental semantic, ontological, and epistemic nature of _____ or morality is (meta-_____), and how moral capacity or moral agency develops and what its nature is (moral psychology.)

   Socrates was one of the first Greek philosophers to encourage both scholars and the common citizen to turn their attention from the outside world to the condition of man. In this view, Knowledge having a bearing on human life was placed highest, all other knowledge being secondary.

   a. ADTECH
   b. ACNielsen
   c. Ethics
   d. AMAX

20. _____ is a broad label that refers to any individuals or households that use goods and services generated within the economy. The concept of a _____ is used in different contexts, so that the usage and significance of the term may vary.

Chapter 8. Information from Respondents: Issues in Data Collection 57

A _____ is a person who uses any product or service.

a. Power III
b. 180SearchAssistant
c. 6-3-5 Brainwriting
d. Consumer

21. _____ is the degree of optimism that consumers feel about the overall state of the economy and their personal financial situation. How confident people feel about stability of their incomes determines their spending activity and therefore serves as one of the key indicators for the overall shape of the economy. In essence, if _____ is higher, consumers are making more purchases, boosting the economic expansion.

a. Cocooning
b. Convenience
c. Gruppi di Acquisto Solidale
d. Consumer Confidence

22. _____ is a telephone surveying technique in which the interviewer follows a script provided by a software application. The software is able to customize the flow of the questionnaire based on the answers provided, as well as information already known about the participant.

CATI may function in the following manner

- A computerized questionnaire is administered to respondents over the telephone.
- The interviewer sits in front of a computer screen
- Upon command, the computer dials the telephone number to be called.
- When contact is made, the interviewer reads the questions posed on the computer screen and records the respondent's answers directly into the computer.
- Interim and update reports can be compiled instantaneously, as the data are being collected.
- CATI software has built-in logic, which also enhances data accuracy.
- The program will personalize questions and control for logically incorrect answers, such as percentage answers that do not add up to 100 percent.
- The software has built-in branching logic, which will skip questions that are not applicable or will probe for more detail when warranted.

a. 6-3-5 Brainwriting
b. Computer-assisted telephone interviewing
c. Power III
d. 180SearchAssistant

23. _____ is that part of statistical practice concerned with the selection of individual observations intended to yield some knowledge about a population of concern, especially for the purposes of statistical inference. Each observation measures one or more properties (weight, location, etc.) of an observable entity enumerated to distinguish objects or individuals.
   a. Richard Buckminster 'Bucky' Fuller
   b. AStore
   c. Sports Marketing Group
   d. Sampling

24. _____ generally refers to a list of all planned expenses and revenues. It is a plan for saving and spending. A _____ is an important concept in microeconomics, which uses a _____ line to illustrate the trade-offs between two or more goods.
   a. Power III
   b. 180SearchAssistant
   c. 6-3-5 Brainwriting
   d. Budget

25. In economics, business, retail, and accounting, a _____ is the value of money that has been used up to produce something, and hence is not available for use anymore. In economics, a _____ is an alternative that is given up as a result of a decision. In business, the _____ may be one of acquisition, in which case the amount of money expended to acquire it is counted as _____.
   a. Marginal cost
   b. Cost
   c. Fixed costs
   d. Transaction cost

Chapter 9. Attitude Measurement

1. _____, a business term, is a measure of how products and services supplied by a company meet or surpass customer expectation. It is seen as a key performance indicator within business and is part of the four perspectives of a Balanced Scorecard.

In a competitive marketplace where businesses compete for customers, _____ is seen as a key differentiator and increasingly has become a key element of business strategy.

   a. Psychological pricing
   b. Safety stock
   c. Street date
   d. Customer satisfaction

2. The '_____' is an expression which typically refers to the theory of scale types developed by the Harvard psychologist Stanley Smith Stevens In this article Stevens claimed that all measurement in science was conducted using four different types of numerical scales which he called 'nominal', 'ordinal', 'interval' and 'ratio'.
   a. Power III
   b. 6-3-5 Brainwriting
   c. 180SearchAssistant
   d. Levels of measurement

3. In grammar, the _____ is the form of an adjective or adverb which denotes the degree or grade by which a person, thing and is used in this context with a subordinating conjunction, such as than, as...as, etc.

The structure of a _____ in English consists normally of the positive form of the adjective or adverb, plus the suffix -er e.g. 'he is taller than his father is', or 'the village is less picturesque than the town nearby'.

   a. Comparative
   b. 6-3-5 Brainwriting
   c. Power III
   d. 180SearchAssistant

4. A _____ is a collection of symbols, experiences and associations connected with a product, a service, a person or any other artifact or entity.

_____s have become increasingly important components of culture and the economy, now being described as 'cultural accessories and personal philosophies'.

Some people distinguish the psychological aspect of a _____ from the experiential aspect.

Chapter 9. Attitude Measurement

a. Naming rights
b. Lovemarks
c. Status brand
d. Brand

5. _____ is a marketing concept that refers to a consumer knowing of a brand's existence; at aggregate (brand) level it refers to the proportion of consumers who know of the brand.

_____ can be measured by showing a consumer the brand and asking whether or not they knew of it beforehand. However, in common market research practice a variety of recognition and recall measures of _____ are employed all of which test the brand name's association to a product category cue, this came about because most market research in the 20th Century was conducted by post or telephone, actually showing the brand to consumers usually required more expensive face-to-face interviews (until web-based interviews became possible.)

a. Store brand
b. Status brand
c. Brand awareness
d. Corporate colours

6. A _____ is a psychometric scale commonly used in questionnaires, and is the most widely used scale in survey research. When responding to a Likert questionnaire item, respondents specify their level of agreement to a statement. The scale is named after its inventor, psychologist Rensis Likert.
   a. Factor analysis
   b. Power III
   c. Semantic differential
   d. Likert scale

7. _____ is a parameter used in sociology, psychology, and other psychometric or behavioral sciences. _____ is demonstrated where a test correlates well with a measure that has previously been validated. The two measures may be for the same construct, or for different, but presumably related, constructs.
   a. Criterion validity
   b. Convergent validity
   c. Concurrent validity
   d. Discriminant validity

Chapter 9. Attitude Measurement

8. In social science and psychometrics, _____ refers to whether a scale measures or correlates with a theorized psychological construct (such as 'fluid intelligence'.) It is related to the theoretical ideas behind the personality trait under consideration; a non-existent concept in the physical sense may be suggested as a method of organising how personality can be viewed. The unobservable idea of a unidimensional easier-to-harder dimension must be 'constructed' in the words of human language and graphics.
   a. Predictive validity
   b. Construct validity
   c. Content validity
   d. Discriminant validity

9. In the absence of a more specific context, convergence denotes the approach toward a definite value, as time goes on; or to a definite point, a common view or opinion, or toward a fixed or equilibrium state. _____ is the adjectival form, and also a noun meaning an iterative approximation.

In mathematics, convergence describes limiting behaviour, particularly of an infinite sequence or series, toward some limit.

   a. Surcharge
   b. Madrid system for the international registration of marks
   c. Convergent
   d. Perceptual maps

10. _____ is the degree to which an operation is similar to (converges on) other operations that it theoretically should also be similar to. For instance, to show the _____ of a test of mathematics skills, the scores on the test can be correlated with scores on other tests that are also designed to measure basic mathematics ability. High correlations between the test scores would be evidence of a _____.
    a. Criterion validity
    b. Discriminant validity
    c. Convergent validity
    d. Predictive validity

11. In psychometrics, _____ is a measure of how well one variable or set of variables predicts an outcome based on information from other variables, and will be achieved if a set of measures from a personality test relate to a behavioral criterion that psychologists agree on. A typical way to achieve this is in relation to the extent to which a score on a personality test can predict future performance or behaviour. Another way involves correlating test scores with another established test that also measures the same personality characteristic.

a. Construct validity
b. Convergent validity
c. Content validity
d. Criterion validity

12. In algebra, the _____ of a polynomial with real or complex coefficients is a certain expression in the coefficients of the polynomial which is equal to zero if and only if the polynomial has a multiple root (i.e. a root with multiplicity greater than one) in the complex numbers. For example, the _____ of the quadratic polynomial

$$ax^2 + bx + c \text{ is } b^2 - 4ac.$$

The _____ of the cubic polynomial

$$ax^3 + bx^2 + cx + d \text{ is } b^2c^2 - 4ac^3 - 4b^3d - 27a^2d^2 + 18abcd.$$

a. Flighting
b. Lifestyle center
c. Consumption Map
d. Discriminant

13. _____ describes the degree to which the operationalization is not similar to (diverges from) other operationalizations that it theoretically should not be similar to.

Campbell and Fiske (1959) introduced the concept of _____ within their discussion on evaluating test validity. They stressed the importance of using both discriminant and convergent validation techniques when assessing new tests.

a. Construct validity
b. Criterion validity
c. Discriminant validity
d. Content validity

14. A _____ is a statement or claim that a particular event will occur in the future in more certain terms than a forecast. The etymology of this word is Latin . In regards to predicting the future Howard H. Stevenson Says, '_____ is at least two things: Important and hard.' Important, because we have to act, and hard because we have to realize the future we want, and what is the best way to get there.

a. Power III
b. 180SearchAssistant
c. 6-3-5 Brainwriting
d. Prediction

15. In psychometrics, _____ is the extent to which a score on a scale or test predicts scores on some criterion measure.

For example, the validity of a cognitive test for job performance is the correlation between test scores and, for example, supervisor performance ratings. Such a cognitive test would have _____ if the observed correlation were statistically significant.

a. Criterion validity
b. Construct validity
c. Convergent validity
d. Predictive validity

Chapter 10. Designing the Questionnaire

1. _____ refer to a collection of facts usually collected as the result of experience, observation or experiment or a set of premises. This may consist of numbers, words particularly as measurements or observations of a set of variables. _____ are often viewed as a lowest level of abstraction from which information and knowledge are derived.
    a. P-Value
    b. Median
    c. Data
    d. Randomization

2. _____ is a term used to describe a process of preparing and collecting data - for example as part of a process improvement or similar project.

_____ usually takes place early on in an improvement project, and is often formalised through a _____ Plan which often contains the following activity.

   1. Pre collection activity - Agree goals, target data, definitions, methods
   2. Collection - _____
   3. Present Findings - usually involves some form of sorting analysis and/or presentation.

A formal _____ process is necessary as it ensures that data gathered is both defined and accurate and that subsequent decisions based on arguments embodied in the findings are valid . The process provides both a baseline from which to measure from and in certain cases a target on what to improve. Types of _____ 1-By mail questionnaires 2-By personal interview

- Six sigma
- Sampling (statistics)

   a. 6-3-5 Brainwriting
   b. Power III
   c. 180SearchAssistant
   d. Data collection

3. A _____ is a research instrument consisting of a series of questions and other prompts for the purpose of gathering information from respondents. Although they are often designed for statistical analysis of the responses, this is not always the case. The _____ was invented by Sir Francis Galton.
    a. Market research
    b. Questionnaire
    c. Mystery shoppers
    d. Mystery shopping

Chapter 10. Designing the Questionnaire

4. _____ in organizations and public policy is both the organizational process of creating and maintaining a plan; and the psychological process of thinking about the activities required to create a desired goal on some scale. As such, it is a fundamental property of intelligent behavior. This thought process is essential to the creation and refinement of a plan, or integration of it with other plans, that is, it combines forecasting of developments with the preparation of scenarios of how to react to them.
   a. Planning
   b. Power III
   c. 180SearchAssistant
   d. 6-3-5 Brainwriting

5. In common law systems that rely on testimony by witnesses, a _____ is a question that suggests the answer or contains the information the examiner is looking for. For example, this question is leading:

   - You were at Duffy's bar on the night of July 15, weren't you?

It suggests that the witness was at Duffy's bar on the night in question. The same question in a non-leading form would be:

   - Where were you on the night of July 15?

This form of question does not suggest to the witness the answer the examiner hopes to elicit.

_____s may often be answerable with a yes or no (though not all yes-no questions are leading), while non-_____s are open-ended. Depending on the circumstances _____s can be objectionable or proper.

   a. Leading question
   b. Contract price
   c. Power III
   d. Substantive law

6. _____ is a standard point of view or personal prejudice. especially when the tendency interferes with the ability to be impartial, unprejudiced, or objective. The term _____ed is used to describe an action, judgment, or other outcome influenced by a prejudged perspective.
   a. Bias
   b. 6-3-5 Brainwriting
   c. Power III
   d. 180SearchAssistant

7. _____ is a compliance tactic that involves getting a person to agree to a large request by first setting them up by having that person agree to a modest request.

In an early study, a team of psychologists telephoned housewives in California and asked if the women would answer a few questions about the household products they used. Three days later, the psychologists called again.

   a. Power III
   b. 180SearchAssistant
   c. Foot-in-the-door technique
   d. 6-3-5 Brainwriting

8. A _____ is a collection of symbols, experiences and associations connected with a product, a service, a person or any other artifact or entity.

_____s have become increasingly important components of culture and the economy, now being described as 'cultural accessories and personal philosophies'.

Some people distinguish the psychological aspect of a _____ from the experiential aspect.

   a. Status brand
   b. Lovemarks
   c. Brand
   d. Naming rights

9. _____ refers to the marketing effects or outcomes that accrue to a product with its brand name compared with those that would accrue if the same product did not have the brand name . And, at the root of these marketing effects is consumers' knowledge. In other words, consumers' knowledge about a brand makes manufacturers/advertisers respond differently or adopt appropriately adapt measures for the marketing of the brand .
   a. Brand implementation
   b. Brand management
   c. Brand equity
   d. Trade Symbols

10. _____, a business term, is a measure of how products and services supplied by a company meet or surpass customer expectation. It is seen as a key performance indicator within business and is part of the four perspectives of a Balanced Scorecard.

In a competitive marketplace where businesses compete for customers, _____ is seen as a key differentiator and increasingly has become a key element of business strategy.

a. Customer satisfaction
b. Street date
c. Safety stock
d. Psychological pricing

Chapter 11. Sampling Fundamentals

1. _____ refer to a collection of facts usually collected as the result of experience, observation or experiment or a set of premises. This may consist of numbers, words particularly as measurements or observations of a set of variables. _____ are often viewed as a lowest level of abstraction from which information and knowledge are derived.
   a. Randomization
   b. P-Value
   c. Median
   d. Data

2. _____ is a term used to describe a process of preparing and collecting data - for example as part of a process improvement or similar project.

   _____ usually takes place early on in an improvement project, and is often formalised through a _____ Plan which often contains the following activity.

   1. Pre collection activity - Agree goals, target data, definitions, methods
   2. Collection - _____
   3. Present Findings - usually involves some form of sorting analysis and/or presentation.

   A formal _____ process is necessary as it ensures that data gathered is both defined and accurate and that subsequent decisions based on arguments embodied in the findings are valid . The process provides both a baseline from which to measure from and in certain cases a target on what to improve. Types of _____ 1-By mail questionnaires 2-By personal interview

   - Six sigma
   - Sampling (statistics)

   a. Power III
   b. 6-3-5 Brainwriting
   c. 180SearchAssistant
   d. Data collection

3. 'Speaking generally, properties are those physical quantities which directly describe the physical attributes of the system; _____s are those combinations of the properties which suffice to determine the response of the system. Properties can have all sorts of dimensions, depending upon the system being considered; _____s are dimensionless, or have the dimension of time or its reciprocal.'

   The term can also be used in engineering contexts, however, as it is typically used in the physical sciences.

   When the terms formal _____ and actual _____ are used, they generally correspond with the definitions used in computer science.

a. 6-3-5 Brainwriting
b. Power III
c. 180SearchAssistant
d. Parameter

4. _____ is that part of statistical practice concerned with the selection of individual observations intended to yield some knowledge about a population of concern, especially for the purposes of statistical inference. Each observation measures one or more properties (weight, location, etc.) of an observable entity enumerated to distinguish objects or individuals.
   a. Richard Buckminster 'Bucky' Fuller
   b. AStore
   c. Sports Marketing Group
   d. Sampling

5. In statistics, _____ or estimation error is the error caused by observing a sample instead of the whole population.

An estimate of a quantity of interest, such as an average or percentage, will generally be subject to sample-to-sample variation. These variations in the possible sample values of a statistic can theoretically be expressed as _____s, although in practice the exact _____ is typically unknown.

   a. Power III
   b. Two-tailed test
   c. Varimax rotation
   d. Sampling error

6. Sampling is the use of a subset of the population to represent the whole population. Probability sampling, or random sampling, is a sampling technique in which the probability of getting any particular sample may be calculated. _____ does not meet this criterion and should be used with caution.
   a. Snowball sampling
   b. Power III
   c. Quota sampling
   d. Nonprobability sampling

7. _____ is a way of expressing knowledge or belief that an event will occur or has occurred. In mathematics the concept has been given an exact meaning in _____ theory, that is used extensively in such areas of study as mathematics, statistics, finance, gambling, science, and philosophy to draw conclusions about the likelihood of potential events and the underlying mechanics of complex systems.

Chapter 11. Sampling Fundamentals

   a. Correlation
   b. Probability
   c. Standard score
   d. Mean

8. In statistics, a simple random sample is a subset of individuals (a sample) chosen from a larger set (a population.) Each individual is chosen randomly and entirely by chance, such that each individual has the same probability of being chosen at any stage during the sampling process, and each subset of k individuals has the same probability of being chosen for the sample as any other subset of k individuals (.) This process and technique is known as _____, and should not be confused with Random Sampling.
   a. Preference regression
   b. Simple random sampling
   c. Marketing research
   d. Cross tabulation

9. In statistics, _____ is a method of sampling from a population.

When sub-populations vary considerably, it is advantageous to sample each subpopulation (stratum) independently. Stratification is the process of grouping members of the population into relatively homogeneous subgroups before sampling.

   a. Linear regression
   b. Frequency distribution
   c. Variance
   d. Stratified sampling

10. _____ is a sampling technique used when 'natural' groupings are evident in a statistical population. It is often used in marketing research. In this technique, the total population is divided into these groups (or clusters) and a sample of the groups is selected.
   a. Snowball sampling
   b. Nonprobability sampling
   c. Power III
   d. Cluster sampling

11. _____ is a statistical method involving the selection of elements from an ordered sampling frame. The most common form of _____ is an equal-probability method, in which every k^{th} element in the frame is selected, where k, the sampling interval (sometimes known as the 'skip'), is calculated as:

sample size (n) = population size (N) /k

Using this procedure each element in the population has a known and equal probability of selection. This makes _____ functionally similar to simple random sampling.

a. Systematic sampling
b. Power III
c. Selection bias
d. 180SearchAssistant

12. _____ is anything that is intended to save time, energy or frustration. A _____ store at a petrol station, for example, sells items that have nothing to do with gasoline/petrol, but it saves the consumer from having to go to a grocery store. '_____' is a very relative term and its meaning tends to change over time.

a. Multidimensional scaling
b. Demographic profile
c. Consumer confidence
d. Convenience

13. _____ is a type of nonprobability sampling which involves the sample being drawn from that part of the population which is close to hand. That is, a sample population selected because it is readily available and convenient. The researcher using such a sample cannot scientifically make generalizations about the total population from this sample because it would not be representative enough.

a. Accidental sampling
b. ADTECH
c. ACNielsen
d. AMAX

14. In _____, the population is first segmented into mutually exclusive sub-groups, just as in stratified sampling. Then judgment is used to select the subjects or units from each segment based on a specified proportion. For example, an interviewer may be told to sample 200 females and 300 males between the age of 45 and 60.

a. Snowball sampling
b. Power III
c. Nonprobability sampling
d. Quota sampling

Chapter 11. Sampling Fundamentals

15. In social science research, _____ is a technique for developing a research sample where existing study subjects recruit future subjects from among their acquaintances. Thus the sample group appears to grow like a rolling snowball. As the sample builds up, enough data is gathered to be useful for research.
    a. Power III
    b. Quota sampling
    c. Snowball sampling
    d. Nonprobability sampling

16. In statistics, _____ has two related meanings:

    - the arithmetic _____
    - the expected value of a random variable, which is also called the population _____.

    It is sometimes stated that the '_____' _____s average. This is incorrect if '_____' is taken in the specific sense of 'arithmetic _____' as there are different types of averages: the _____, median, and mode. For instance, average house prices almost always use the median value for the average. These three types of averages are all measures of locations.

    a. Mean
    b. Null hypothesis
    c. Confounding variables
    d. Standard score

17. In mathematics and statistics, the arithmetic mean (or simply the mean) of a list of numbers is the sum of all of the list divided by the number of items in the list. If the list is a statistical population, then the mean of that population is called a population mean. If the list is a statistical sample, we call the resulting statistic a _____.
    a. Probability
    b. Sample size
    c. Statistics
    d. Sample mean

18. The _____ of a statistical sample is the number of observations that constitute it. It is typically denoted n, a positive integer (natural number.)

Typically, all else being equal, a larger _____ leads to increased precision in estimates of various properties of the population.

Chapter 11. Sampling Fundamentals

a. Statistics
b. Statistical inference
c. Control chart
d. Sample size

19. _____ is one of the four elements of marketing mix. An organization or set of organizations (go-betweens) involved in the process of making a product or service available for use or consumption by a consumer or business user.

The other three parts of the marketing mix are product, pricing, and promotion.

a. Better Living Through Chemistry
b. Clustering
c. LIFO
d. Distribution

20. In statistics, _____ is a simple measure of the variability or dispersion of a data set. A low _____ indicates that the data points tend to be very close to the same value (the mean), while high _____ indicates that the data are 'spread out' over a large range of values.

For example, the average height for adult men in the United States is about 70 inches, with a _____ of around 3 inches.

a. Probability
b. Stratified sampling
c. Statistically significant
d. Standard deviation

21. _____ generally refers to a list of all planned expenses and revenues. It is a plan for saving and spending. A _____ is an important concept in microeconomics, which uses a _____ line to illustrate the trade-offs between two or more goods.

a. Power III
b. 6-3-5 Brainwriting
c. 180SearchAssistant
d. Budget

22. A number of different _____s are indicated below.

- Randomized controlled trial
    - Double-blind randomized trial
    - Single-blind randomized trial
    - Non-blind trial
- Nonrandomized trial (quasi-experiment)
    - Interrupted time series design (measures on a sample or a series of samples from the same population are obtained several times before and after a manipulated event or a naturally occurring event) - considered a type of quasi-experiment

- Cohort study
    - Prospective cohort
    - Retrospective cohort
    - Time series study
- Case-control study
    - Nested case-control study
- Cross-sectional study
    - Community survey (a type of cross-sectional study)

When choosing a _____, many factors must be taken into account. Different types of studies are subject to different types of bias. For example, recall bias is likely to occur in cross-sectional or case-control studies where subjects are asked to recall exposure to risk factors.

a. Study design
b. Longitudinal studies
c. 180SearchAssistant
d. Power III

23. In probability theory and statistics, the _____ of a random variable, probability distribution, or sample is a measure of statistical dispersion, averaging the squared distance of its possible values from the expected value (mean.) Whereas the mean is a way to describe the location of a distribution, the _____ is a way to capture its scale or degree of being spread out. The unit of _____ is the square of the unit of the original variable.

a. Statistical hypothesis test
b. Variance
c. Survey research
d. Confounding variables

24. _____ is a standard point of view or personal prejudice. especially when the tendency interferes with the ability to be impartial, unprejudiced, or objective. The term _____ed is used to describe an action, judgment, or other outcome influenced by a prejudged perspective.

a. 180SearchAssistant
b. Power III
c. 6-3-5 Brainwriting
d. Bias

25. _____ is defined by the American _____ Association as the activity, set of institutions, and processes for creating, communicating, delivering, and exchanging offerings that have value for customers, clients, partners, and society at large. The term developed from the original meaning which referred literally to going to market, as in shopping, or going to a market to sell goods or services.

_____ practice tends to be seen as a creative industry, which includes advertising, distribution and selling.

a. Business marketing
b. Product naming
c. Gatefold
d. Marketing

26. Consumer market research is a form of applied sociology that concentrates on understanding the behaviours, whims and preferences, of consumers in a market-based economy, and aims to understand the effects and comparative success of marketing campaigns. The field of consumer _____ as a statistical science was pioneered by Arthur Nielsen with the founding of the ACNielsen Company in 1923.

Thus _____ is the systematic and objective identification, collection, analysis, and dissemination of information for the purpose of assisting management in decision making related to the identification and solution of problems and opportunities in marketing.

a. Marketing research
b. Logit analysis
c. Simple random sampling
d. Market analysis

27. In population genetics and population ecology, _____ is the number of individual organisms in a population.

The effective _____ (N_e) is defined as 'the number of breeding individuals in an idealized population that would show the same amount of dispersion of allele frequencies under random genetic drift or the same amount of inbreeding as the population under consideration.' N_e is usually less than N (the absolute _____) and this has important applications in conservation genetics.

Small _____ results in increased genetic drift.

a. Power III
b. Population size
c. 6-3-5 Brainwriting
d. 180SearchAssistant

28. In statistics, a _____ is a tabulation of the values that one or more variables take in a sample.

Univariate _____s are often presented as lists, ordered by quantity, showing the number of times each value appears. For example, if 100 people rate a five-point Likert scale assessing their agreement with a statement on a scale on which 1 denotes strong agreement and 5 strong disagreement, the _____ of their responses might look like:

This simple tabulation has two drawbacks.

a. Median
b. Linear regression
c. Standard normal distribution
d. Frequency distribution

29. In probability theory and statistics, the _____ is a normalized measure of dispersion of a probability distribution. It is defined as the ratio of the standard deviation σ to the mean μ:

$$c_v = \frac{\sigma}{\mu}$$

This is only defined for non-zero mean, and is most useful for variables that are always positive. It is also known as unitized risk.

a. P-Value
b. Stratified sampling
c. Sample mean
d. Coefficient of variation

30. _____ is the examining of goods or services from retailers with the intent to purchase at that time. _____ is an activity of selection and/or purchase. In some contexts it is considered a leisure activity as well as an economic one.

a. Discount store
b. Khodebshchik
c. Shopping
d. Hawkers

Chapter 12. Fundamentals of Data Analysis

1. _____ refer to a collection of facts usually collected as the result of experience, observation or experiment or a set of premises. This may consist of numbers, words particularly as measurements or observations of a set of variables. _____ are often viewed as a lowest level of abstraction from which information and knowledge are derived.
   a. P-Value
   b. Randomization
   c. Median
   d. Data

2. _____ is a process of gathering, modeling, and transforming data with the goal of highlighting useful information, suggesting conclusions, and supporting decision making. _____ has multiple facets and approaches, encompassing diverse techniques under a variety of names, in different business, science, and social science domains.

   Data mining is a particular _____ technique that focuses on modeling and knowledge discovery for predictive rather than purely descriptive purposes.

   a. Power III
   b. 180SearchAssistant
   c. 6-3-5 Brainwriting
   d. Data analysis

3. In probability theory and statistics, _____ indicates the strength and direction of a linear relationship between two random variables. That is in contrast with the usage of the term in colloquial speech, denoting any relationship, not necessarily linear. In general statistical usage, _____ or co-relation refers to the departure of two random variables from independence.
   a. Stratified sampling
   b. Standard normal distribution
   c. Correlation
   d. Type I error

4. The process of _____ involves emphasising some aspects of a phenomenon, or of a set of data -- giving them 'more weight' in the final effect or result. It is analogous to the practice of adding extra weight to one side of a pair of scales to favour a buyer or seller.

   While _____ may be applied to a set of data, for example epidemiological data, it is more commonly applied to measurements of light, heat, sound, gamma radiation, in fact any stimulus that is spread over a spectrum of frequencies.

Chapter 12. Fundamentals of Data Analysis

a. 180SearchAssistant
b. 6-3-5 Brainwriting
c. Power III
d. Weighting

5. In statistics, econometrics, epidemiology and related disciplines, the method of _____ is used to estimate causal relationships when controlled experiments are not feasible.

Statistically, _____ methods allow consistent estimation when the explanatory variables (covariates) are correlated with the error terms. Such correlation may occur when the dependent variable causes at least one of the of covariates ('reverse' causation), when there are relevant explanatory variables which are omitted from the model, or when the covariates are subject to measurement error.

a. AMAX
b. ACNielsen
c. Instrumental variables
d. ADTECH

6. _____s are used in open sentences. For instance, in the formula x + 1 = 5, x is a _____ which represents an 'unknown' number. _____s are often represented by letters of the Roman alphabet, or those of other alphabets, such as Greek, and use other special symbols.

a. Variable
b. Market specialization
c. Sample sales
d. Quantitative

7. In statistics, a _____ is a tabulation of the values that one or more variables take in a sample.

Univariate _____s are often presented as lists, ordered by quantity, showing the number of times each value appears. For example, if 100 people rate a five-point Likert scale assessing their agreement with a statement on a scale on which 1 denotes strong agreement and 5 strong disagreement, the _____ of their responses might look like:

This simple tabulation has two drawbacks.

a. Linear regression
b. Standard normal distribution
c. Median
d. Frequency distribution

8. _____ are used to describe the basic features of the data gathered from an experimental study in various ways. A _____ is distinguished from inductive statistics. They provide simple summaries about the sample and the measures.
   a. Statistics
   b. Probability
   c. Data
   d. Descriptive statistics

9. _____ is one of the four elements of marketing mix. An organization or set of organizations (go-betweens) involved in the process of making a product or service available for use or consumption by a consumer or business user.

The other three parts of the marketing mix are product, pricing, and promotion.

   a. LIFO
   b. Better Living Through Chemistry
   c. Clustering
   d. Distribution

10. _____ is a mathematical science pertaining to the collection, analysis, interpretation or explanation, and presentation of data. It also provides tools for prediction and forecasting based on data. It is applicable to a wide variety of academic disciplines, from the natural and social sciences to the humanities, government and business.
   a. Type I error
   b. Statistics
   c. Variance
   d. Randomization

11. A _____ is a plan of action designed to achieve a particular goal.

_____ is different from tactics. In military terms, tactics is concerned with the conduct of an engagement while _____ is concerned with how different engagements are linked.

Chapter 12. Fundamentals of Data Analysis

a. 180SearchAssistant
b. 6-3-5 Brainwriting
c. Power III
d. Strategy

12. In statistics, _____ has two related meanings:

    - the arithmetic _____
    - the expected value of a random variable, which is also called the population _____.

It is sometimes stated that the '_____' _____s average. This is incorrect if '_____' is taken in the specific sense of 'arithmetic _____' as there are different types of averages: the _____, median, and mode. For instance, average house prices almost always use the median value for the average. These three types of averages are all measures of locations.

a. Mean
b. Confounding variables
c. Null hypothesis
d. Standard score

13. In mathematics and statistics, the arithmetic mean (or simply the mean) of a list of numbers is the sum of all of the list divided by the number of items in the list. If the list is a statistical population, then the mean of that population is called a population mean. If the list is a statistical sample, we call the resulting statistic a _____.
    a. Sample size
    b. Statistics
    c. Probability
    d. Sample mean

14. _____ is that part of statistical practice concerned with the selection of individual observations intended to yield some knowledge about a population of concern, especially for the purposes of statistical inference. Each observation measures one or more properties (weight, location, etc.) of an observable entity enumerated to distinguish objects or individuals.
    a. AStore
    b. Richard Buckminster 'Bucky' Fuller
    c. Sampling
    d. Sports Marketing Group

Chapter 12. Fundamentals of Data Analysis

15. The '_____' is an expression which typically refers to the theory of scale types developed by the Harvard psychologist Stanley Smith Stevens In this article Stevens claimed that all measurement in science was conducted using four different types of numerical scales which he called 'nominal', 'ordinal', 'interval' and 'ratio'.
    a. 6-3-5 Brainwriting
    b. Levels of measurement
    c. Power III
    d. 180SearchAssistant

16. An example of a repeated measures _____ would be if one group were pre- and post-tested. (This example occurs in education quite frequently.) If a teacher wanted to examine the effect of a new set of textbooks on student achievement, (s)he could test the class at the beginning of the year (pretest) and at the end of the year (posttest.)
    a. Standard deviation
    b. T-test
    c. Statistics
    d. Sample mean

17. In statistics, _____ is a collection of statistical models, and their associated procedures, in which the observed variance is partitioned into components due to different explanatory variables. The initial techniques of the _____ were developed by the statistician and geneticist R. A. Fisher in the 1920s and 1930s, and is sometimes known as Fisher's ANOVA or Fisher's _____, due to the use of Fisher's F-distribution as part of the test of statistical significance.

There are three conceptual classes of such models:

1. Fixed-effects models assumes that the data came from normal populations which may differ only in their means. (Model 1)
2. Random effects models assume that the data describe a hierarchy of different populations whose differences are constrained by the hierarchy. (Model 2)
3. Mixed-effect models describe situations where both fixed and random effects are present. (Model 3)

In practice, there are several types of ANOVA depending on the number of treatments and the way they are applied to the subjects in the experiment:

- One-way ANOVA is used to test for differences among two or more independent groups. Typically, however, the One-way ANOVA is used to test for differences among at least three groups, since the two-group case can be covered by a T-test (Gossett, 1908.)

a. ACNielsen
b. Analysis of variance
c. Arithmetic mean
d. Interval estimation

18. In statistics, a _____ is a dimensionless quantity derived by subtracting the population mean from an individual raw score and then dividing the difference by the population standard deviation. This conversion process is called standardizing or normalizing; however, 'normalizing' can refer to many types of ratios; see normalization (statistics) for more.

Yhey are also called z-values, z-scores, normal scores, and standardized variables; the use of 'Z' is because the normal distribution is also known as the 'Z distribution'.

a. Statistical hypothesis test
b. Type I error
c. Data
d. Standard score

19. In probability theory and statistics, the _____ of a random variable, probability distribution, or sample is a measure of statistical dispersion, averaging the squared distance of its possible values from the expected value (mean.) Whereas the mean is a way to describe the location of a distribution, the _____ is a way to capture its scale or degree of being spread out. The unit of _____ is the square of the unit of the original variable.

a. Statistical hypothesis test
b. Survey research
c. Confounding variables
d. Variance

20. A _____ is any statistical test for which the distribution of the test statistic under the null hypothesis can be approximated by a normal distribution. Since many test statistics are approximately normally distributed for large samples (due to the central limit theorem), many statistical tests can be performed as approximate _____s if the sample size is not too small. In addition, some statistical tests such as comparisons of means between two samples, or a comparison of the mean of one sample to a given constant, are exact _____s under certain assumptions.

a. Variance
b. Confidence interval
c. Z-test
d. Linear regression

21. In statistics, _____ is used for two things;

- to construct a simple formula that will predict what value will occur for a quantity of interest when other related variables take given values.
- to allow a test to be made of whether a given variable does have an effect on a quantity of interest in situations where there may be many related variables.

In both cases, several sets of outcomes are available for the quantity of interest together with the related variables.

_____ is a form of regression analysis in which the relationship between one or more independent variables and another variable, called the dependent variable, is modelled by a least squares function, called a _____ equation. This function is a linear combination of one or more model parameters, called regression coefficients. A _____ equation with one independent variable represents a straight line when the predicted value (i.e. the dependant variable from the regression equation) is plotted against the independent variable: this is called a simple _____.

a. Control chart
b. Probability sampling
c. Data
d. Linear regression

22. In statistics, _____ is a collective name for techniques for the modeling and analysis of numerical data consisting of values of a dependent variable and of one or more independent variables The dependent variable in the regression equation is modeled as a function of the independent variables, corresponding parameters, and an error term. The error term is treated as a random variable.
a. Multicollinearity
b. Regression analysis
c. Variance inflation factor
d. Stepwise regression

23. _____ is a computer program used for statistical analysis.

_____ (originally, Statistical Package for the Social Sciences) was released in its first version in 1968 after being founded by Norman Nie and C. Hadlai Hull. Nie was then a political science postgraduate at Stanford University, and now Research Professor in the Department of Political Science at Stanford and Professor Emeritus of Political Science at the University of Chicago.

a. SPSS
b. Power III
c. 6-3-5 Brainwriting
d. 180SearchAssistant

Chapter 13. Hypothesis Testing

1. _____ refer to a collection of facts usually collected as the result of experience, observation or experiment or a set of premises. This may consist of numbers, words particularly as measurements or observations of a set of variables. _____ are often viewed as a lowest level of abstraction from which information and knowledge are derived.
   a. Median
   b. P-Value
   c. Randomization
   d. Data

2. _____ is a process of gathering, modeling, and transforming data with the goal of highlighting useful information, suggesting conclusions, and supporting decision making. _____ has multiple facets and approaches, encompassing diverse techniques under a variety of names, in different business, science, and social science domains.

Data mining is a particular _____ technique that focuses on modeling and knowledge discovery for predictive rather than purely descriptive purposes.

   a. 180SearchAssistant
   b. Power III
   c. 6-3-5 Brainwriting
   d. Data analysis

3. In probability theory and statistics, _____ indicates the strength and direction of a linear relationship between two random variables. That is in contrast with the usage of the term in colloquial speech, denoting any relationship, not necessarily linear. In general statistical usage, _____ or co-relation refers to the departure of two random variables from independence.
   a. Standard normal distribution
   b. Type I error
   c. Stratified sampling
   d. Correlation

4. The _____ and the null hypothesis are the two rival hypotheses whose likelihoods are compared by a statistical hypothesis test. Usually the _____ is the possibility that an observed effect is genuine and the null hypothesis is the rival possibility that it has resulted from chance.

The classical (or frequentist) approach is to calculate the probability that the observed effect (or one more extreme) will occur if the null hypothesis is true.

Chapter 13. Hypothesis Testing

a. Alternative hypothesis
b. Interval estimation
c. ACNielsen
d. Analysis of variance

5. In statistical hypothesis testing, the _____ formally describes some aspect of the statistical behaviour of a set of data; this description is treated as valid unless the actual behaviour of the data contradicts this assumption. Thus, the _____ is contrasted against another hypothesis. Statistical hypothesis testing is used to make a decision about whether the data contradicts the _____: this is called significance testing.

a. Data
b. Null hypothesis
c. Stratified sampling
d. T-test

6. _____ is one of the four elements of marketing mix. An organization or set of organizations (go-betweens) involved in the process of making a product or service available for use or consumption by a consumer or business user.

The other three parts of the marketing mix are product, pricing, and promotion.

a. LIFO
b. Distribution
c. Clustering
d. Better Living Through Chemistry

7. In statistics, a _____ is a tabulation of the values that one or more variables take in a sample.

Univariate _____s are often presented as lists, ordered by quantity, showing the number of times each value appears. For example, if 100 people rate a five-point Likert scale assessing their agreement with a statement on a scale on which 1 denotes strong agreement and 5 strong disagreement, the _____ of their responses might look like:

This simple tabulation has two drawbacks.

a. Standard normal distribution
b. Median
c. Frequency distribution
d. Linear regression

Chapter 13. Hypothesis Testing

8. In statistics, _____ has two related meanings:

   - the arithmetic _____
   - the expected value of a random variable, which is also called the population _____.

   It is sometimes stated that the '_____' _____s average. This is incorrect if '_____' is taken in the specific sense of 'arithmetic _____' as there are different types of averages: the _____, median, and mode. For instance, average house prices almost always use the median value for the average. These three types of averages are all measures of locations.

   a. Mean
   b. Null hypothesis
   c. Standard score
   d. Confounding variables

9. The _____ of a test is a traditional frequentist statistical hypothesis testing concept. In simple cases, it is defined as the probability of making a decision to reject the null hypothesis when the null hypothesis is actually true (a decision known as a Type I error, or 'false positive determination'.) The decision is often made using the p-value: if the p-value is less than the _____, then the null hypothesis is rejected.
   a. Statistics
   b. Significance level
   c. Standard normal distribution
   d. Z-test

10. In probability theory and statistics, the _____ of a random variable, probability distribution, or sample is a measure of statistical dispersion, averaging the squared distance of its possible values from the expected value (mean.) Whereas the mean is a way to describe the location of a distribution, the _____ is a way to capture its scale or degree of being spread out. The unit of _____ is the square of the unit of the original variable.
    a. Survey research
    b. Variance
    c. Confounding variables
    d. Statistical hypothesis test

11. A personal and cultural _____ is a relative ethic _____, an assumption upon which implementation can be extrapolated. A _____ system is a set of consistent _____s and measures that is soo not true. A principle _____ is a foundation upon which other _____s and measures of integrity are based.

Chapter 13. Hypothesis Testing

a. Private branding
b. Customization
c. Dolly Dimples
d. Value

12. In statistics, the terms _____ and type II error are used to describe possible errors made in a statistical decision process. In 1928, Jerzy Neyman (1894-1981) and Egon Pearson (1895-1980), both eminent statisticians, discussed the problems associated with 'deciding whether or not a particular sample may be judged as likely to have been randomly drawn from a certain population' (1928/1967, p.1): and identified 'two sources of error', namely:

Type I (>α): reject the null-hypothesis when the null-hypothesis is true, and
Type II (>β): fail to reject the null-hypothesis when the null-hypothesis is false

In 1930, they elaborated on these two sources of error, remarking that 'in testing hypotheses two considerations must be kept in view, (1) we must be able to reduce the chance of rejecting a true hypothesis to as low a value as desired; (2) the test must be so devised that it will reject the hypothesis tested when it is likely to be false'

Scientists recognize two different sorts of error:

- Statistical error: the difference between a computed, estimated specified and inherently unpredictable fluctuations in the measurement apparatus or the system being studied.
- Systematic error: the difference between a computed, estimated specified and which, once identified, can usually be eliminated.

Statisticians speak of two significant sorts of statistical error. The context is that there is a 'null hypothesis' which corresponds to a presumed default 'state of nature', e.g., that an individual is free of disease, that an accused is innocent that is, that the individual has the disease, that the accused is guilty, or that the login candidate is an authorized user.

a. Data
b. Mean
c. Type I error
d. Standard score

13. The _____ is a statistical test used in inference, in which a given statistical hypothesis will be rejected when the value of the statistic is either sufficiently small or sufficiently large. The test is named after the 'tail' of data under the far left and far right of a bell-shaped normal data distribution, or bell curve. However, the terminology is extended to tests relating to distributions other than normal.

a. Power III
b. Varimax rotation
c. Two-tailed test
d. Sampling error

14. In probability theory and statistics, the _____ (or expectation value or mean and for continuous random variables with a density function it is the probability density -weighted integral of the possible values.

The term '_____' can be misleading.

a. Expected value
b. AMAX
c. ACNielsen
d. ADTECH

15. In probability theory and statistics, the _____ is one of the most widely used theoretical probability distributions in inferential statistics, e.g., in statistical significance tests. It is useful because, under reasonable assumptions, easily calculated quantities can be proven to have distributions that approximate to the _____ if the null hypothesis is true.

The best-known situations in which the _____ are used are the common chi-square tests for goodness of fit of an observed distribution to a theoretical one, and of the independence of two criteria of classification of qualitative data.

a. Scientific controls
b. Second Life
c. Mystery shoppers
d. Chi-square distribution

16. In probability theory and statistics, the _____ is a discrete probability distribution that expresses the probability of a number of events occurring in a fixed period of time if these events occur with a known average rate and independently of the time since the last event. The _____ can also be used for the number of events in other specified intervals such as distance, area or volume.

The distribution was discovered by Sim>éon-Denis Poisson (1781-1840) and published, together with his probability theory, in 1838 in his work Recherches sur la probabilit>é des jugements en mati>ères criminelles et mati>ère civile ('Research on the Probability of Judgments in Criminal and Civil Matters'.)

a. Book of business
b. Complex sale
c. Sexism,
d. Poisson distribution

17. In statistics, a _____ is a dimensionless quantity derived by subtracting the population mean from an individual raw score and then dividing the difference by the population standard deviation. This conversion process is called standardizing or normalizing; however, 'normalizing' can refer to many types of ratios; see normalization (statistics) for more.

Yhey are also called z-values, z-scores, normal scores, and standardized variables; the use of 'Z' is because the normal distribution is also known as the 'Z distribution'.

a. Type I error
b. Data
c. Statistical hypothesis test
d. Standard score

18. In statistics, _____ is a simple measure of the variability or dispersion of a data set. A low _____ indicates that the data points tend to be very close to the same value (the mean), while high _____ indicates that the data are 'spread out' over a large range of values.

For example, the average height for adult men in the United States is about 70 inches, with a _____ of around 3 inches.

a. Probability
b. Stratified sampling
c. Standard deviation
d. Statistically significant

19. An example of a repeated measures _____ would be if one group were pre- and post-tested. (This example occurs in education quite frequently.) If a teacher wanted to examine the effect of a new set of textbooks on student achievement, (s)he could test the class at the beginning of the year (pretest) and at the end of the year (posttest.)
a. Statistics
b. Sample mean
c. Standard deviation
d. T-test

Chapter 13. Hypothesis Testing

20. In statistics, a _____ is an interval estimate of a population parameter. Instead of estimating the parameter by a single value, an interval likely to include the parameter is given. Thus, _____s are used to indicate the reliability of an estimate.
    a. Statistics
    b. Null hypothesis
    c. Standard normal distribution
    d. Confidence interval

21. In statistics, _____ is a collection of statistical models, and their associated procedures, in which the observed variance is partitioned into components due to different explanatory variables. The initial techniques of the _____ were developed by the statistician and geneticist R. A. Fisher in the 1920s and 1930s, and is sometimes known as Fisher's ANOVA or Fisher's _____, due to the use of Fisher's F-distribution as part of the test of statistical significance.

There are three conceptual classes of such models:

1. Fixed-effects models assumes that the data came from normal populations which may differ only in their means. (Model 1)
2. Random effects models assume that the data describe a hierarchy of different populations whose differences are constrained by the hierarchy. (Model 2)
3. Mixed-effect models describe situations where both fixed and random effects are present. (Model 3)

In practice, there are several types of ANOVA depending on the number of treatments and the way they are applied to the subjects in the experiment:

- One-way ANOVA is used to test for differences among two or more independent groups. Typically, however, the One-way ANOVA is used to test for differences among at least three groups, since the two-group case can be covered by a T-test (Gossett, 1908.)

    a. Arithmetic mean
    b. Analysis of variance
    c. Interval estimation
    d. ACNielsen

22. In statistics, the dependent/independent variable terminology is used more widely than just in relation to controlled experiments. For example the data analysis of two jointly varying quantities may involve treating each in turn as the dependent variable and the other as the independent variable. However, for general usage, the pair _____ and explanatory variable is preferable as quantities treated as 'independent variables' are rarely statistically independent.

a. 180SearchAssistant
b. Power III
c. Field experiment
d. Response variable

23. _____s are used in open sentences. For instance, in the formula x + 1 = 5, x is a _____ which represents an 'unknown' number. _____s are often represented by letters of the Roman alphabet, or those of other alphabets, such as Greek, and use other special symbols.
a. Quantitative
b. Market specialization
c. Sample sales
d. Variable

24. _____ in economics and business is the result of an exchange and from that trade we assign a numerical monetary value to a good, service or asset. If I trade 4 apples for an orange, the _____ of an orange is 4 - apples. Inversely, the _____ of an apple is 1/4 oranges.
a. Transfer pricing
b. Price war
c. Contribution margin-based pricing
d. Price

25. In statistics, analysis of variance (_____) is a collection of statistical models, and their associated procedures, in which the observed variance is partitioned into components due to different explanatory variables. In its simplest form _____ gives a statistical test of whether the means of several groups are all equal, and therefore generalizes Student's two-sample t-test to more than two groups.

There are three conceptual classes of such models:

1. Fixed-effects models assumes that the data came from normal populations which may differ only in their means. (Model 1)
2. Random effects models assume that the data describe a hierarchy of different populations whose differences are constrained by the hierarchy. (Model 2)
3. Mixed-effect models describe situations where both fixed and random effects are present. (Model 3)

In practice, there are several types of _____ depending on the number of treatments and the way they are applied to the subjects in the experiment:

- One-way _____ is used to test for differences among two or more independent groups. Typically, however, the one-way _____ is used to test for differences among at least three groups, since the two-group case can be covered by a T-test (Gossett, 1908.)

a. ANOVA
b. ACNielsen
c. AMAX
d. ADTECH

Chapter 14. Correlation Analysis and Regression Analysis

1. In probability theory and statistics, _____ indicates the strength and direction of a linear relationship between two random variables. That is in contrast with the usage of the term in colloquial speech, denoting any relationship, not necessarily linear. In general statistical usage, _____ or co-relation refers to the departure of two random variables from independence.
    a. Stratified sampling
    b. Type I error
    c. Standard normal distribution
    d. Correlation

2. _____ refer to a collection of facts usually collected as the result of experience, observation or experiment or a set of premises. This may consist of numbers, words particularly as measurements or observations of a set of variables. _____ are often viewed as a lowest level of abstraction from which information and knowledge are derived.
    a. Median
    b. P-Value
    c. Randomization
    d. Data

3. _____ is a process of gathering, modeling, and transforming data with the goal of highlighting useful information, suggesting conclusions, and supporting decision making. _____ has multiple facets and approaches, encompassing diverse techniques under a variety of names, in different business, science, and social science domains.

    Data mining is a particular _____ technique that focuses on modeling and knowledge discovery for predictive rather than purely descriptive purposes.

    a. Power III
    b. 180SearchAssistant
    c. Data analysis
    d. 6-3-5 Brainwriting

4. In statistics, _____ is a collective name for techniques for the modeling and analysis of numerical data consisting of values of a dependent variable and of one or more independent variables The dependent variable in the regression equation is modeled as a function of the independent variables, corresponding parameters, and an error term. The error term is treated as a random variable.
    a. Stepwise regression
    b. Regression analysis
    c. Multicollinearity
    d. Variance inflation factor

5. In statistics, _____ is used for two things;

Chapter 14. Correlation Analysis and Regression Analysis

- to construct a simple formula that will predict what value will occur for a quantity of interest when other related variables take given values.
- to allow a test to be made of whether a given variable does have an effect on a quantity of interest in situations where there may be many related variables.

In both cases, several sets of outcomes are available for the quantity of interest together with the related variables.

_____ is a form of regression analysis in which the relationship between one or more independent variables and another variable, called the dependent variable, is modelled by a least squares function, called a _____ equation. This function is a linear combination of one or more model parameters, called regression coefficients. A _____ equation with one independent variable represents a straight line when the predicted value (i.e. the dependant variable from the regression equation) is plotted against the independent variable: this is called a simple _____.

a. Data
b. Control chart
c. Probability sampling
d. Linear regression

6. In statistics, the _____ is a common measure of the correlation (linear dependence) between two variables X and Y. It is very widely used in the sciences as a measure of the strength of linear dependence between two variables, giving a value somewhere between +1 and -1 inclusive. It was first introduced by Francis Galton in the 1880s, and named after Karl Pearson.

In accordance with the usual convention, when calculated for an entire population, the Pearson product-moment correlation is typically designated by the analogous Greek letter, which in this case is ρ.

a. Pearson product-moment correlation coefficient
b. Probability
c. Control chart
d. Confidence interval

7. Sample mean and _____ are statistics computed from a collection of data, thought of as being random.

Chapter 14. Correlation Analysis and Regression Analysis 97

Given a random sample [x] from an [x]-dimensional random variable [x] (i.e., realizations of [x] independent random variables with the same distribution as [x]), the sample mean is

[x]

In coordinates, writing the vectors as columns,

[x]

the entries of the sample mean are

[x]

The _____ of [x] is the n-by-n matrix [x] with the entries given by

[x]

The sample mean and the _____ matrix are unbiased estimates of the mean and the covariance matrix of the random variable [x]. The reason why the _____ matrix has [x] in the denominator rather than [x] is essentially that the population mean E(X) is not known and is replaced by the sample mean [x].

  a. Power III
  b. Sample covariance
  c. 180SearchAssistant
  d. Canonical correlation analysis

8. In statistics, _____ or Spearman's rho is a non-parametric measure of correlation - that is, it assesses how well an arbitrary monotonic function could describe the relationship between two variables, without making any other assumptions about the particular nature of the relationship between the variables. Certain other measures of correlation are parametric in the sense of being based on possible relationships of a parameterised form, such as a linear relationship.

In principle, >ρ is simply a special case of the Pearson product-moment coefficient in which two sets of data X_i and Y_i are converted to rankings x_i and y_i before calculating the coefficient.

a. Sample sales
b. Good things come to those who wait
c. Spearman's rank correlation coefficient
d. PlattForm, Inc.

9. _____s are used in open sentences. For instance, in the formula x + 1 = 5, x is a _____ which represents an 'unknown' number. _____s are often represented by letters of the Roman alphabet, or those of other alphabets, such as Greek, and use other special symbols.
   a. Sample sales
   b. Market specialization
   c. Variable
   d. Quantitative

10. 'Speaking generally, properties are those physical quantities which directly describe the physical attributes of the system; _____s are those combinations of the properties which suffice to determine the response of the system. Properties can have all sorts of dimensions, depending upon the system being considered; _____s are dimensionless, or have the dimension of time or its reciprocal.'

The term can also be used in engineering contexts, however, as it is typically used in the physical sciences.

When the terms formal _____ and actual _____ are used, they generally correspond with the definitions used in computer science.

   a. 6-3-5 Brainwriting
   b. 180SearchAssistant
   c. Power III
   d. Parameter

11. _____ is a computer program used for statistical analysis.

_____ (originally, Statistical Package for the Social Sciences) was released in its first version in 1968 after being founded by Norman Nie and C. Hadlai Hull. Nie was then a political science postgraduate at Stanford University, and now Research Professor in the Department of Political Science at Stanford and Professor Emeritus of Political Science at the University of Chicago.

Chapter 14. Correlation Analysis and Regression Analysis 99

a. 180SearchAssistant
b. 6-3-5 Brainwriting
c. Power III
d. SPSS

12. In statistics, _____ has two related meanings:

- the arithmetic _____
- the expected value of a random variable, which is also called the population _____.

It is sometimes stated that the '_____' _____s average. This is incorrect if '_____' is taken in the specific sense of 'arithmetic _____' as there are different types of averages: the _____, median, and mode. For instance, average house prices almost always use the median value for the average. These three types of averages are all measures of locations.

a. Standard score
b. Mean
c. Null hypothesis
d. Confounding variables

13. In statistics, the _____ or _____ of an estimator is one of many ways to quantify the amount by which an estimator differs from the true value of the quantity being estimated. As a loss function, _____ is called squared error loss. _____ measures the average of the square of the 'error.' The error is the amount by which the estimator differs from the quantity to be estimated.

a. 6-3-5 Brainwriting
b. Power III
c. Mean squared error
d. 180SearchAssistant

14. The terms '_____' and 'independent variable' are used in similar but subtly different ways in mathematics and statistics as part of the standard terminology in those subjects. They are used to distinguish between two types of quantities being considered, separating them into those available at the start of a process and those being created by it, where the latter (_____s) are dependent on the former (independent variables.)

In traditional calculus, a function is defined as a relation between two terms called variables because their values vary.

a. Dependent variable
b. 180SearchAssistant
c. Field experiment
d. Power III

15. In statistics, the _____, R^2 is used in the context of statistical models whose main purpose is the prediction of future outcomes on the basis of other related information. It is the proportion of variability in a data set that is accounted for by the statistical model. It provides a measure of how well future outcomes are likely to be predicted by the model.
    a. Variance inflation factor
    b. Multicollinearity
    c. Regression analysis
    d. Coefficient of determination

16. A _____ is a method of making statistical decisions using experimental data. It is sometimes called confirmatory data analysis, in contrast to exploratory data analysis. In frequency probability, these decisions are almost always made using null-hypothesis tests; that is, ones that answer the question Assuming that the null hypothesis is true, what is the probability of observing a value for the test statistic that is at least as extreme as the value that was actually observed? One use of hypothesis testing is deciding whether experimental results contain enough information to cast doubt on conventional wisdom.
    a. Pearson product-moment correlation coefficient
    b. Significance level
    c. Control chart
    d. Statistical hypothesis test

17. An example of a repeated measures _____ would be if one group were pre- and post-tested. (This example occurs in education quite frequently.) If a teacher wanted to examine the effect of a new set of textbooks on student achievement, (s)he could test the class at the beginning of the year (pretest) and at the end of the year (posttest.)
    a. Statistics
    b. T-test
    c. Sample mean
    d. Standard deviation

18. In statistics, _____ includes regression models in which the choice of predictive variables is carried out by an automatic procedure. Usually, this takes the form of a sequence of F-tests, but other techniques are possible, such as t-tests, adjusted R-square, Akaike information criterion, Bayesian information criterion, Mallows' Cp, or false discovery rate. In this example from engineering, necessity and sufficiency are usually determined by F-tests.

a. Stepwise regression
b. Multicollinearity
c. Regression analysis
d. Variance inflation factor

1. _____ is a fee paid on borrowed assets. It is the price paid for the use of borrowed money, or, money earned by deposited funds. Assets that are sometimes lent with _____ include money, shares, consumer goods through hire purchase, major assets such as aircraft, and even entire factories in finance lease arrangements.
    a. ADTECH
    b. ACNielsen
    c. AMAX
    d. Interest

Chapter 16. Applications of Marketing Research

1. _____ is defined by the American _____ Association as the activity, set of institutions, and processes for creating, communicating, delivering, and exchanging offerings that have value for customers, clients, partners, and society at large. The term developed from the original meaning which referred literally to going to market, as in shopping, or going to a market to sell goods or services.

_____ practice tends to be seen as a creative industry, which includes advertising, distribution and selling.

a. Marketing
b. Product naming
c. Business marketing
d. Gatefold

2. Consumer market research is a form of applied sociology that concentrates on understanding the behaviours, whims and preferences, of consumers in a market-based economy, and aims to understand the effects and comparative success of marketing campaigns. The field of consumer _____ as a statistical science was pioneered by Arthur Nielsen with the founding of the ACNielsen Company in 1923 .

Thus _____ is the systematic and objective identification, collection, analysis, and dissemination of information for the purpose of assisting management in decision making related to the identification and solution of problems and opportunities in marketing.

a. Simple random sampling
b. Market analysis
c. Logit analysis
d. Marketing research

3. _____ is a business management strategy aimed at embedding awareness of quality in all organizational processes. _____ has been widely used in manufacturing, education, call centers, government, and service industries, as well as NASA space and science programs.

When used together as a phrase, the three words in this expression have the following meanings:

- Total: Involving the entire organization, supply chain, and/or product life cycle
- Quality: With its usual definitions, with all its complexities
- Management: The system of managing with steps like Plan, Organize, Control, Lead, Staff, provisioning and organizing.

Chapter 16. Applications of Marketing Research

As defined by the International Organization for Standardization (ISO):

'_____ is a management approach for an organization, centered on quality, based on the participation of all its members and aiming at long-term success through customer satisfaction, and benefits to all members of the organization and to society.' ISO 8402:1994

One major aim is to reduce variation from every process so that greater consistency of effort is obtained. (Royse, D., Thyer, B., Padgett D., ' Logan T., 2006)

In Japan, _____ comprises four process steps, namely:

1. Kaizen - Focuses on 'Continuous Process Improvement', to make processes visible, repeatable and measurable.
2. Atarimae Hinshitsu - The idea that 'things will work as they are supposed to' .
3. Kansei - Examining the way the user applies the product leads to improvement in the product itself.
4. Miryokuteki Hinshitsu - The idea that 'things should have an aesthetic quality' (for example, a pen will write in a way that is pleasing to the writer.)

_____ requires that the company maintain this quality standard in all aspects of its business. This requires ensuring that things are done right the first time and that defects and waste are eliminated from operations.

a. 6-3-5 Brainwriting
b. 180SearchAssistant
c. Power III
d. Total Quality Management

4. A _____ is a collection of symbols, experiences and associations connected with a product, a service, a person or any other artifact or entity.

_____s have become increasingly important components of culture and the economy, now being described as 'cultural accessories and personal philosophies'.

Some people distinguish the psychological aspect of a _____ from the experiential aspect.

a. Naming rights
b. Status brand
c. Brand
d. Lovemarks

Chapter 16. Applications of Marketing Research

5. _____ refers to the marketing effects or outcomes that accrue to a product with its brand name compared with those that would accrue if the same product did not have the brand name. And, at the root of these marketing effects is consumers' knowledge. In other words, consumers' knowledge about a brand makes manufacturers/advertisers respond differently or adopt appropriately adapt measures for the marketing of the brand.

   a. Brand management
   b. Trade Symbols
   c. Brand implementation
   d. Brand equity

6. In the art of selling, _____ is one stage in a seven stage personal selling process.

In this stage the salesperson takes a qualified prospect through a series of question and answer sessions in order to identify the requirements of the prospect. During this step, the salesperson will attempt to help the buyer identify and quantify a business need or a 'gap' between where the client is today and where they would like to be in the future.

   a. 180SearchAssistant
   b. Power III
   c. Product churning
   d. Need identification

7. _____ is systematic determination of merit, worth, and significance of something or someone using criteria against a set of standards. _____ often is used to characterize and appraise subjects of interest in a wide range of human enterprises, including the arts, criminal justice, foundations and non-profit organizations, government, health care, and other human services.

Depending on the topic of interest, there are professional groups which look to the quality and rigor of the _____ process.

   a. ACNielsen
   b. Evaluation
   c. AMAX
   d. ADTECH

8. Defined narrowly, a _____ is one who claims to experience a vision or apparition connected to the supernatural. At times this involves seeing into the future. The _____ state is achieved via meditation, drugs, lucid dreams, day dreams, or art.

a. 6-3-5 Brainwriting
b. 180SearchAssistant
c. Visionary
d. Power III

9. _____ is one of the four Ps of the marketing mix. The other three aspects are product, promotion, and place. It is also a key variable in microeconomic price allocation theory.

a. Transfer pricing
b. Pricing
c. Resale price maintenance
d. Cost-plus pricing

10. A _____, in the field of business and marketing, is a geographic region or demographic group used to gauge the viability of a product or service in the mass market prior to a wide scale roll-out. The criteria used to judge the acceptability of a _____ region or group include:

1. a population that is demographically similar to the proposed target market; and
2. relative isolation from densely populated media markets so that advertising to the test audience can be efficient and economical.

The _____ ideally aims to duplicate 'everything' - promotion and distribution as well as `product' - on a smaller scale. The technique replicates, typically in one area, what is planned to occur in a national launch; and the results are very carefully monitored, so that they can be extrapolated to projected national results. The `area' may be any one of the following:

- Television area
- Test town
- Residential neighborhood
- Test site

A number of decisions have to be taken about any _____:

- Which _____?
- What is to be tested?
- How long a test?
- What are the success criteria?

The simple go or no-go decision, together with the related reduction of risk, is normally the main justification for the expense of _____s. At the same time, however, such _____s can be used to test specific elements of a new product's marketing mix; possibly the version of the product itself, the promotional message and media spend, the distribution channels and the price.

a. Test market
b. Preadolescence
c. Power III
d. 180SearchAssistant

11. A _____ is a plan of action designed to achieve a particular goal.

_____ is different from tactics. In military terms, tactics is concerned with the conduct of an engagement while _____ is concerned with how different engagements are linked.

a. Power III
b. 180SearchAssistant
c. 6-3-5 Brainwriting
d. Strategy

12. _____ is the pricing technique of setting a relatively low initial entry price, often lower than the eventual market price, to attract new customers. The strategy works on the expectation that customers will switch to the new brand because of the lower price. _____ is most commonly associated with a marketing objective of increasing market share or sales volume, rather than to make profit in the short term.
a. Pricing objectives
b. Penetration pricing
c. Contribution margin-based pricing
d. Competitor indexing

13. _____ is the study of the Earth and its lands, features, inhabitants, and phenomena. A literal translation would be 'to describe or write about the Earth'. The first person to use the word '_____' was Eratosthenes .
a. 6-3-5 Brainwriting
b. 180SearchAssistant
c. Power III
d. Geography

14. _____ is the practice of keeping the price of a product or service artificially high in order to encourage favorable perceptions among buyers, based solely on the price. The practice is intended to exploit the (not necessarily justifiable) tendency for buyers to assume that expensive items enjoy an exceptional reputation or represent exceptional quality and distinction.

The use of _____ as either a marketing strategy or a competitive practice depends on certain factors that influence its profitability and sustainability.

a. Discounts and allowances
b. Price points
c. Competitor indexing
d. Premium pricing

15. _____ in economics and business is the result of an exchange and from that trade we assign a numerical monetary value to a good, service or asset. If I trade 4 apples for an orange, the _____ of an orange is 4 - apples. Inversely, the _____ of an apple is 1/4 oranges.
a. Price
b. Price war
c. Contribution margin-based pricing
d. Transfer pricing

16. _____ is one of the four elements of marketing mix. An organization or set of organizations (go-betweens) involved in the process of making a product or service available for use or consumption by a consumer or business user.

The other three parts of the marketing mix are product, pricing, and promotion.

a. LIFO
b. Clustering
c. Distribution
d. Better Living Through Chemistry

17. A _____ applies the scientific method to experimentally examine an intervention in the real world (or as many experimental economists like to say, naturally-occurring environments) rather than in the laboratory. _____s, like lab experiments, generally randomize subjects (or other sampling units) into treatment and control groups and compare outcomes between these groups. Clinical trials of pharmaceuticals are one example of _____s.
a. 180SearchAssistant
b. Field experiment
c. Response variable
d. Power III

18. A _____ is a commercial building for storage of goods. _____s are used by manufacturers, importers, exporters, wholesalers, transport businesses, customs, etc. They are usually large plain buildings in industrial areas of cities and towns.

a. 6-3-5 Brainwriting
b. Power III
c. Warehouse
d. 180SearchAssistant

19. _____ is a form of communication that typically attempts to persuade potential customers to purchase or to consume more of a particular brand of product or service. 'While now central to the contemporary global economy and the reproduction of global production networks, it is only quite recently that _____ has been more than a marginal influence on patterns of sales and production. The formation of modern _____ was intimately bound up with the emergence of new forms of monopoly capitalism around the end of the 19th and beginning of the 20th century as one element in corporate strategies to create, organize and where possible control markets, especially for mass produced consumer goods.
   a. AMAX
   b. ADTECH
   c. ACNielsen
   d. Advertising

20. _____ is a specialized form of marketing research conducted to improve the efficiency of advertising. According to MarketConscious.com, 'It may focus on a specific ad or campaign, or may be directed at a more general understanding of how advertising works or how consumers use the information in advertising. It can entail a variety of research approaches, including psychological, sociological, economic, and other perspectives.'

1879 - N.W. Ayer conducts custom research in an attempt to win the advertising business of Nichols-Shepard Co., a manufacturer of agricultural machinery.

   a. INVISTA
   b. American Medical Association
   c. Electrolux
   d. Advertising research

21. In economics, business, retail, and accounting, a _____ is the value of money that has been used up to produce something, and hence is not available for use anymore. In economics, a _____ is an alternative that is given up as a result of a decision. In business, the _____ may be one of acquisition, in which case the amount of money expended to acquire it is counted as _____.
   a. Fixed costs
   b. Transaction cost
   c. Cost
   d. Marginal cost

Chapter 16. Applications of Marketing Research

22. _____ involves disseminating information about a product, product line, brand, or company. It is one of the four key aspects of the marketing mix. (The other three elements are product marketing, pricing, and distribution). P>_____ is generally sub-divided into two parts:

- Above the line _____: Promotion in the media (e.g. TV, radio, newspapers, Internet and Mobile Phones) in which the advertiser pays an advertising agency to place the ad
- Below the line _____: All other _____. Much of this is intended to be subtle enough for the consumer to be unaware that _____ is taking place. E.g. sponsorship, product placement, endorsements, sales _____, merchandising, direct mail, personal selling, public relations, trade shows

   a. Cash and carry
   b. M80
   c. Technology maturity lifecycle
   d. Promotion

23. _____ is a form of social influence. It is the process of guiding people toward the adoption of an idea, attitude, or action by rational and symbolic (though not always logical) means. It is strategy of problem-solving relying on 'appeals' rather than coercion.
   a. Persuasion
   b. Power III
   c. 6-3-5 Brainwriting
   d. 180SearchAssistant

24. Human beings are also considered to be _____ because they have the ability to change raw materials into valuable _____. The term Human _____ can also be defined as the skills, energies, talents, abilities and knowledge that are used for the production of goods or the rendering of services. While taking into account human beings as _____, the following things have to be kept in mind:

- The size of the population
- The capabilities of the individuals in that population

Many _____ cannot be consumed in their original form. They have to be processed in order to change them into more usable commodities.

   a. 180SearchAssistant
   b. Resources
   c. Power III
   d. 6-3-5 Brainwriting

Chapter 16. Applications of Marketing Research

25. _____ refers to a business or organization attempting to acquire goods or services to accomplish the goals of the enterprise. Though there are several organizations that attempt to set standards in the _____ process, processes can vary greatly between organizations. Typically the word '_____' is not used interchangeably with the word 'procurement', since procurement typically includes Expediting, Supplier Quality, and Traffic and Logistics (T'L) in addition to _____.
    a. Drop shipping
    b. Supply chain network
    c. Slip sheet
    d. Purchasing

26. _____ is an advertisement in which a particular product specifically mentions a competitor by name for the express purpose of showing why the competitor is inferior to the product naming it.

This should not be confused with parody advertisements, where a fictional product is being advertised for the purpose of poking fun at the particular advertisement, nor should it be confused with the use of a coined brand name for the purpose of comparing the product without actually naming an actual competitor. ('Wikipedia tastes better and is less filling than the Encyclopedia Galactica.')

In the 1980s, during what has been referred to as the cola wars, soft-drink manufacturer Pepsi ran a series of advertisements where people, caught on hidden camera, in a blind taste test, chose Pepsi over rival Coca-Cola.

    a. GL-70
    b. Cost per conversion
    c. Heavy-up
    d. Comparative advertising

27. A _____ is any kind of medical test performed to aid in the diagnosis or detection of disease. For example:

    - to diagnose diseases
    - to measure the progress or recovery from disease
    - to confirm that a person is free from disease

A drug test can be a specific medical test to acertain the presence of a certain drug in the body (for example, in drug addicts.)

Some medical tests are parts of a simple physical examination which require only simple tools in the hands of a skilled practitioner, and can be performed in an office environment. Some other tests require elaborate equipment used by medical technologists or the use of a sterile operating theatre environment.

a. Power III
b. 180SearchAssistant
c. 6-3-5 Brainwriting
d. Diagnostic test

28. In psychology, philosophy, and the cognitive sciences, _____ is the process of attaining awareness or understanding of sensory information. It is a task far more complex than was imagined in the 1950s and 1960s, when it was predicted that building perceiving machines would take about a decade, a goal which is still very far from fruition. The word _____ comes from the Latin words _____, percepio, meaning 'receiving, collecting, action of taking possession, apprehension with the mind or senses.'

_____ is one of the oldest fields in psychology.

a. Groupthink
b. Perception
c. 180SearchAssistant
d. Power III

29. _____ generally refers to a list of all planned expenses and revenues. It is a plan for saving and spending. A _____ is an important concept in microeconomics, which uses a _____ line to illustrate the trade-offs between two or more goods.

a. Budget
b. 6-3-5 Brainwriting
c. Power III
d. 180SearchAssistant

30. _____ psychogalvanic reflex is a method of measuring the electrical resistance of the skin. There has been a long history of electrodermal activity research, most of it dealing with spontaneous fluctuations. Most investigators accept the phenomenon without understanding exactly what it means.

a. 6-3-5 Brainwriting
b. 180SearchAssistant
c. Power III
d. Galvanic skin response

Chapter 16. Applications of Marketing Research

31. A number of different _____s are indicated below.

- Randomized controlled trial
    - Double-blind randomized trial
    - Single-blind randomized trial
    - Non-blind trial
- Nonrandomized trial (quasi-experiment)
    - Interrupted time series design (measures on a sample or a series of samples from the same population are obtained several times before and after a manipulated event or a naturally occurring event) - considered a type of quasi-experiment

- Cohort study
    - Prospective cohort
    - Retrospective cohort
    - Time series study
- Case-control study
    - Nested case-control study
- Cross-sectional study
    - Community survey (a type of cross-sectional study)

When choosing a _____, many factors must be taken into account. Different types of studies are subject to different types of bias. For example, recall bias is likely to occur in cross-sectional or case-control studies where subjects are asked to recall exposure to risk factors.

a. Study design
b. Longitudinal studies
c. 180SearchAssistant
d. Power III

32. A _____ is defined by the International Co-operative Alliance's Statement on the Co-operative Identity as an autonomous association of persons united voluntarily to meet their common economic, social, and cultural needs and aspirations through a jointly-owned and democratically-controlled enterprise. It is a business organization owned and operated by a group of individuals for their mutual benefit. A _____ may also be defined as a business owned and controlled equally by the people who use its services or who work at it.

a. 180SearchAssistant
b. Power III
c. 6-3-5 Brainwriting
d. Cooperative

33. _____ is an American firm that measures media audiences, including television, radio, theatre films (via the AMC MAP program) and newspapers. _____, headquartered in New York City and operating primarily from Chicago, is best-known for the Nielsen Ratings, a measurement of television viewership.

114 *Chapter 16. Applications of Marketing Research*

_____, the preeminent media research company in the world, began as a division of ACNielsen, a marketing research firm.

a. Superbrands
b. Zany Brainy
c. Coinstar
d. Nielsen Media Research

34. _____ is one of the four aspects of promotional mix. (The other three parts of the promotional mix are advertising, personal selling, and publicity/public relations.) Media and non-media marketing communication are employed for a pre-determined, limited time to increase consumer demand, stimulate market demand or improve product availability.

a. New Media Strategies
b. Word of mouth
c. Merchandising
d. Sales promotion

35. A _____ is a type of business entity in which partners (owners) share with each other the profits or losses of the business undertaking in which all have invested. _____s are often favored over corporations for taxation purposes, as the _____ structure does not generally incur a tax on profits before it is distributed to the partners (i.e. there is no dividend tax levied.) However, depending on the _____ structure and the jurisdiction in which it operates, owners of a _____ may be exposed to greater personal liability than they would as shareholders of a corporation.

a. Screener
b. Partnership
c. Colour trademark
d. Contributory negligence

36. Competitiveness is a comparative concept of the ability and performance of a firm, sub-sector or country to sell and supply goods and/or services in a given market. Although widely used in economics and business management, the usefulness of the concept, particularly in the context of national competitiveness, is vigorously disputed by economists, such as Paul Krugman .

The term may also be applied to markets, where it is used to refer to the extent to which the market structure may be regarded as perfectly _____.

a. Free trade zone
b. Geographical pricing
c. Customs union
d. Competitive

37. _____ is, in very basic words, a position a firm occupies against its competitors.

According to Michael Porter, the three methods for creating a sustainable _____ are through:

1. Cost leadership - Cost advantage occurs when a firm delivers the same services as its competitors but at a lower cost;

2.

a. 6-3-5 Brainwriting
b. Power III
c. 180SearchAssistant
d. Competitive advantage

38. _____ is a marketing concept that refers to a consumer knowing of a brand's existence; at aggregate (brand) level it refers to the proportion of consumers who know of the brand.

_____ can be measured by showing a consumer the brand and asking whether or not they knew of it beforehand. However, in common market research practice a variety of recognition and recall measures of _____ are employed all of which test the brand name's association to a product category cue, this came about because most market research in the 20th Century was conducted by post or telephone, actually showing the brand to consumers usually required more expensive face-to-face interviews (until web-based interviews became possible.)

a. Store brand
b. Corporate colours
c. Brand awareness
d. Status brand

39. _____, in marketing, consists of a consumer's commitment to repurchase the brand and can be demonstrated by repeated buying of a product or service or other positive behaviors such as word of mouth advocacy. True _____ implies that the consumer is willing, at least on occasion, to put aside their own desires in the interest of the brand. _____ has been proclaimed by some to be the ultimate goal of marketing.

Chapter 16. Applications of Marketing Research

    a. Naming rights
    b. Brandable software
    c. Branded entertainment
    d. Brand loyalty

40. _____ or brand stretching is a marketing strategy in which a firm marketing a product with a well-developed image uses the same brand name in a different product category. Organizations use this strategy to increase and leverage brand equity (definition: the net worth and long-term sustainability just from the renowned name.) An example of a _____ is Jello-gelatin creating Jello pudding pops.
    a. Web 2.0
    b. Trade Symbols
    c. Visual merchandising
    d. Brand extension

41. _____, a business term, is a measure of how products and services supplied by a company meet or surpass customer expectation. It is seen as a key performance indicator within business and is part of the four perspectives of a Balanced Scorecard.

In a competitive marketplace where businesses compete for customers, _____ is seen as a key differentiator and increasingly has become a key element of business strategy.

    a. Customer satisfaction
    b. Safety stock
    c. Psychological pricing
    d. Street date

42. A _____ is a research instrument consisting of a series of questions and other prompts for the purpose of gathering information from respondents. Although they are often designed for statistical analysis of the responses, this is not always the case. The _____ was invented by Sir Francis Galton.
    a. Market research
    b. Mystery shoppers
    c. Questionnaire
    d. Mystery shopping

43. _____ is that area of marketing research which focuses on customers' perceptions with their shopping or purchase experience.

Chapter 16. Applications of Marketing Research

Many firms are interested in understanding what their customers thought about their shopping or purchase experience, because finding new customers is generally more costly and difficult that servicing existing or repeat customers.

Many people are familiar with 'business to customer' (B2C) or retail-level research, but there are also many 'business to business' (B2B) or wholesale-level projects commissioned as well.

   a. 180SearchAssistant
   b. Power III
   c. 6-3-5 Brainwriting
   d. Customer satisfaction research

44. _____ is a term used to describe any service or product for which the non-essential features have been removed. The use of the term 'frills' refers to a style of fabric decoration. Something offered to customers for no additional charge may be designated as a 'frill' - for example, free drinks on airline journeys, or a radio installed in a rental car.
   a. 6-3-5 Brainwriting
   b. Power III
   c. No frills
   d. 180SearchAssistant

45. A _____ is a structured collection of records or data that is stored in a computer system. The structure is achieved by organizing the data according to a _____ model. The model in most common use today is the relational model.
   a. 180SearchAssistant
   b. 6-3-5 Brainwriting
   c. Power III
   d. Database

46. _____ is a form of direct marketing using databases of customers or potential customers to generate personalized communications in order to promote a product or service for marketing purposes. The method of communication can be any addressable medium, as in direct marketing.

The distinction between direct and _____ stems primarily from the attention paid to the analysis of data.

   a. Database marketing
   b. Power III
   c. Direct marketing
   d. Direct Marketing Associations

Chapter 16. Applications of Marketing Research

47. _____ , according to Cornish, 'the process of acquiring and analyzing information in order to understand the market (both existing and potential customers); to determine the current and future needs and preferences, attitudes and behavior of the market; and to assess changes in the business environment that may affect the size and nature of the market in the future.' ('Product', 1997, p147.)

This figure shows how the interaction between variables from producers, communication channels, and consumers vary the effectiveness of _____ which affects the performance of the sales of a new product. The product is central in a circle because it helps to direct what information is gathered and how.

a. Specialty catalogs
b. Brand parity
c. Market intelligence
d. Co-branding

48. _____ is a broad label that refers to any individuals or households that use goods and services generated within the economy. The concept of a _____ is used in different contexts, so that the usage and significance of the term may vary.

A _____ is a person who uses any product or service.

a. 180SearchAssistant
b. 6-3-5 Brainwriting
c. Power III
d. Consumer

49. _____ refer to a collection of facts usually collected as the result of experience, observation or experiment or a set of premises. This may consist of numbers, words particularly as measurements or observations of a set of variables. _____ are often viewed as a lowest level of abstraction from which information and knowledge are derived.
a. Randomization
b. Data
c. Median
d. P-Value

50. _____ refers to the additional value of a commodity over the cost of commodities used to produce it from the previous stage of production. An example is the price of gasoline at the pump over the price of the oil in it. In national accounts used in macroeconomics, it refers to the contribution of the factors of production, i.e., land, labor, and capital goods, to raising the value of a product and corresponds to the incomes received by the owners of these factors. The factors of production provide 'services' which raise the unit price of a product (X) relative to the cost per unit of intermediate goods used up in the production of X. _____ is shared between the factors of production (capital, labor, also human capital), giving rise to issues of distribution.

a. Deregulation
b. Power III
c. Value added
d. Consumer spending

51. Electronic commerce, commonly known as _____ or eCommerce, consists of the buying and selling of products or services over electronic systems such as the Internet and other computer networks. The amount of trade conducted electronically has grown extraordinarily with wide-spread Internet usage. A wide variety of commerce is conducted in this way, spurring and drawing on innovations in electronic funds transfer, supply chain management, Internet marketing, online transaction processing, electronic data interchange (EDI), inventory management systems, and automated data collection systems.
   a. E-commerce
   b. ACNielsen
   c. AMAX
   d. ADTECH

52. In marketing, customer _____, lifetime customer value (LCV), or _____ (LTV) and a new concept of 'customer life cycle management' is the present value of the future cash flows attributed to the customer relationship. Use of customer _____ as a marketing metric tends to place greater emphasis on customer service and long-term customer satisfaction, rather than on maximizing short-term sales.

Customer _____ has intuitive appeal as a marketing concept, because in theory it represents exactly how much each customer is worth in monetary terms, and therefore exactly how much a marketing department should be willing to spend to acquire each customer.

   a. Commercial planning
   b. Cannibalization
   c. Marketing strategy
   d. Lifetime value

53. A personal and cultural _____ is a relative ethic _____, an assumption upon which implementation can be extrapolated. A _____ system is a set of consistent _____s and measures that is soo not true. A principle _____ is a foundation upon which other _____s and measures of integrity are based.
   a. Dolly Dimples
   b. Value
   c. Customization
   d. Private branding

Chapter 16. Applications of Marketing Research

54. _____ is an independent technology and market research company that provides its clients with advice about technology's impact on business and consumers. _____ has four research centers in the US: Cambridge, Massachusetts; Foster City, California; Washington, D.C.; and Westport, Connecticut. It also has four European research centers in Amsterdam, Frankfurt, London, and Paris.
   a. Checkoff
   b. Forrester Research
   c. National Asset Recovery Services
   d. Mapinfo

55. _____ is a form of marketing developed from direct response marketing campaigns conducted in the 1970's and 1980's which emphasizes customer retention and satisfaction, rather than a dominant focus on 'point of sale' transactions.

   _____ differs from other forms of marketing in that it recognizes the long term value to the firm of keeping customers, as opposed to direct or 'Intrusion' marketing, which focuses upon acquisition of new clients by targeting majority demographics based upon prospective client lists.

   _____ refers to long-term and mutually beneficial arrangement wherein both buyer and seller focus on value enhancement through the certain of more satisfying exchange. This approach attempts to transcend the simple purchase exchange process with customer to make more meaningful and richer contact by providing a more holistic, personalized purchase, and use orn consumption experience to create stronger ties.

   a. Global marketing
   b. Relationship marketing
   c. Cause-related Marketing
   d. Digital marketing

56. _____ is a computer program used for statistical analysis.

   _____ (originally, Statistical Package for the Social Sciences) was released in its first version in 1968 after being founded by Norman Nie and C. Hadlai Hull. Nie was then a political science postgraduate at Stanford University, and now Research Professor in the Department of Political Science at Stanford and Professor Emeritus of Political Science at the University of Chicago.

   a. 6-3-5 Brainwriting
   b. Power III
   c. 180SearchAssistant
   d. SPSS

57. In statistics, _____ is used for two things;

- to construct a simple formula that will predict what value will occur for a quantity of interest when other related variables take given values.
- to allow a test to be made of whether a given variable does have an effect on a quantity of interest in situations where there may be many related variables.

In both cases, several sets of outcomes are available for the quantity of interest together with the related variables.

_____ is a form of regression analysis in which the relationship between one or more independent variables and another variable, called the dependent variable, is modelled by a least squares function, called a _____ equation. This function is a linear combination of one or more model parameters, called regression coefficients. A _____ equation with one independent variable represents a straight line when the predicted value (i.e. the dependant variable from the regression equation) is plotted against the independent variable: this is called a simple _____.

a. Linear regression
b. Probability sampling
c. Control chart
d. Data

58. In statistics, _____ is a collective name for techniques for the modeling and analysis of numerical data consisting of values of a dependent variable and of one or more independent variables The dependent variable in the regression equation is modeled as a function of the independent variables, corresponding parameters, and an error term. The error term is treated as a random variable.
    a. Stepwise regression
    b. Multicollinearity
    c. Variance inflation factor
    d. Regression analysis

ANSWER KEY

Chapter 1
1. c   2. d   3. b   4. d   5. c   6. b   7. d   8. b   9. c   10. a
11. d   12. d   13. d   14. d   15. d   16. d   17. d   18. b   19. c

Chapter 2
1. c   2. c   3. d   4. b   5. a   6. d   7. c   8. d   9. d   10. c
11. b   12. d   13. d   14. c   15. d   16. d

Chapter 3
1. d   2. c   3. c   4. d   5. d   6. c   7. d   8. c

Chapter 4
1. d   2. a   3. d   4. d   5. d   6. b   7. d   8. b   9. c   10. d
11. d   12. d   13. c   14. d   15. c   16. a   17. d   18. d   19. d   20. c
21. d   22. d   23. d   24. d   25. b   26. a   27. c   28. d   29. d   30. d
31. b

Chapter 5
1. b   2. b   3. d   4. d   5. a   6. a   7. a   8. a   9. d   10. c
11. d   12. a   13. a   14. c   15. a   16. c   17. d   18. b   19. d   20. d
21. a   22. b   23. d   24. c   25. d   26. b   27. b   28. c   29. b   30. b
31. d   32. d   33. b   34. d

Chapter 6
1. d   2. d   3. b   4. d   5. c   6. a   7. d   8. d   9. d   10. d
11. b   12. c   13. b   14. a   15. d   16. a   17. c   18. a   19. a   20. d
21. b

Chapter 7
1. b   2. a   3. d   4. d   5. b   6. b   7. d   8. d   9. a   10. b
11. b   12. a   13. a   14. d   15. c   16. b   17. a   18. c   19. d   20. d
21. c   22. d   23. d

Chapter 8
1. d   2. c   3. d   4. d   5. c   6. c   7. a   8. d   9. d   10. d
11. d   12. d   13. d   14. d   15. a   16. d   17. c   18. d   19. c   20. d
21. d   22. b   23. d   24. d   25. b

Chapter 9
1. d   2. d   3. a   4. d   5. c   6. d   7. c   8. b   9. c   10. c
11. d   12. d   13. c   14. d   15. d

Chapter 10
1. c   2. d   3. b   4. a   5. a   6. a   7. c   8. c   9. c   10. a

ANSWER KEY

Chapter 11
1. d	2. d	3. d	4. d	5. d	6. d	7. b	8. b	9. d	10. d
11. a	12. d	13. a	14. d	15. c	16. a	17. d	18. d	19. d	20. d
21. d	22. a	23. b	24. d	25. d	26. a	27. b	28. d	29. d	30. c

Chapter 12
1. d	2. d	3. c	4. d	5. c	6. a	7. d	8. d	9. d	10. b
11. d	12. a	13. d	14. c	15. b	16. b	17. b	18. d	19. d	20. c
21. d	22. b	23. a							

Chapter 13
1. d	2. d	3. d	4. a	5. b	6. b	7. c	8. a	9. b	10. b
11. d	12. c	13. c	14. a	15. d	16. d	17. d	18. c	19. d	20. d
21. b	22. d	23. d	24. d	25. a					

Chapter 14
1. d	2. d	3. c	4. b	5. d	6. a	7. b	8. c	9. c	10. d
11. d	12. b	13. c	14. a	15. d	16. d	17. b	18. a		

Chapter 15
1. d

Chapter 16
1. a	2. d	3. d	4. c	5. d	6. d	7. b	8. c	9. b	10. a
11. d	12. b	13. d	14. d	15. a	16. c	17. b	18. c	19. d	20. d
21. c	22. d	23. a	24. b	25. d	26. d	27. d	28. b	29. a	30. d
31. a	32. d	33. d	34. d	35. b	36. d	37. d	38. c	39. d	40. d
41. a	42. c	43. d	44. c	45. d	46. a	47. c	48. d	49. b	50. c
51. a	52. d	53. b	54. b	55. b	56. d	57. a	58. d		

www.ingramcontent.com/pod-product-compliance
Lightning Source LLC
Chambersburg PA
CBHW082047230426
43670CB00016B/2812